Tanya B. Ditto

Shar-Pei

Everything About Purchase, Care,
Nutrition, Behavior, and Training

Filled with Full-color Photographs

Illustrations by Michele Earle-Bridges

BARRON'S

CONTENTS

MEET THE CHINESE SHAR-PEI

In 1978, the Guinness Book of World Records listed the Chinese Shar-Pei (sah-pay) as the rarest dog in the world. Fortunately for the breed, that record is theirs no longer. The recovery was a success story unmatched in history.

Rescue of a Vanishing Breed

In May 1971, an article in an American magazine, accompanied by a photograph of the "last surviving Chinese Shar-Pei," laid the foundation for a consuming and continuing public interest. Even so, although readers were aware that the breed had all but disappeared, these concerned animal lovers could do little to help. It was not until April 1973 that a second article was published outlining a plan that would eventually prove the savior of the breed. Matgo Law, a young breeder in Hong Kong, centered his article around an urgent appeal for American sponsors. Mr. Law asked readers to assist in the rescue of the last scattered representatives of the Shar-Pei by importing them to kennels in this country.

The Chinese Shar-Pei was accepted into the AKC Non-Sporting group in 1992.

Underscoring Mr. Law's appeal was the knowledge that the Crown Colony of Hong Kong, under British dominion for 99 years, was scheduled to revert to Chinese control by the year 1997. It was the Chinese government, breeders recalled, that with a series of taxes and bans already had eliminated such "decadent, bourgeois luxuries" as dogs from mainland China.

As was to be expected, as word of the appeal spread, dog lovers responded in even greater number than candidates could be found.

By mid-1991, emerging from a nucleus of fewer than one hundred registrants, the Chinese Shar-Pei Club of America (CSPCA) had registered over 70,000 dogs. Those numbers are growing every year. On May 4, 1988, Shar-Pei were accepted into the Miscellaneous Class of the American Kennel Club (AKC), the first step toward full registration. On October 8, 1991, the American Kennel Club officially recognized the

The Shar-Pei was once known as the Oriental Gladiator.

Chinese Shar-Pei by accepting the breed into the Non-Sporting group effective January 1, 1992.

Origin

Known to some as the sharkskin dog, to others as the Oriental fighting dog, or simply the Chinese bulldog, the Shar-Pei is an ancient breed that can trace its ancestors back 2,000 years.

An agile, muscular dog, the Shar-Pei is commonly thought to be related to the Chow Chow, for generations the principal sporting dog of China. The Shar-Pei and the Chow Chow do have in common a bluish-purple tongue, a trait not shared with any other dog. Indeed, until the Shar-Pei resurfaced, the Chow Chow was thought to be the only breed in the world with this particular color tongue.

In part because of its appearance, and in part due to its Chow Chow heritage, the Shar-Pei is indelibly linked to the giant mastiff breeds. The structure of the Shar-Pei head, in particular, reminds many of the ancient British and German mastiffs, warrior dogs noted for their powerful jaws and for the strength of their neck muscles.

The Fighting Dog

At one time in its history the Chinese Shar-Pei breed was considered a fighting dog. Fierce, armored dogs went into battle with the Roman legions. In the Middle Ages, trained dogs carried cauldrons of flaming resin to their masters on the front lines. Dogfighting, bullbaiting, and bearbaiting were accepted sports well into the nineteenth century.

SHAR-PEI SOUNDBITES

Clay statuettes dating from China's Han Dynasty (approx. 200 B.C. to A.D. 200), preserved in Asian Art Museum collections, clearly depict our rugged, tail-wheeled "Tomb Dog."

When the original, provisional, standard of the Hong Kong and Kowloon Kennel Association (HKKA) arrived in the United States shortly after the first rescued dogs, it was packed with references to the breed's warlike skills. The HKKA standard described the Shar-Pei as having "all the features of a gladiator," for instance. The perfect stance was said to be as impressive as the "calm and firm stature of a severe warrior." The "sunken small eyes," for example, apparently were bred deliberately to reduce the "chance of injury." The tiny ears "small as possible," minimized the "opportunity of his opponent" to achieve or retain its grip. Those curved canine teeth increased the "difficulty of freeing the grip."

The Shar-Pei as a Hunter

The stamina and determination of the Shar-Pei are equally evident in tales of its hunting capabilities. Shar-Pei guarded homes in rural areas, functioned as herders for the farmer, and when necessary, harassed and expelled wild animals.

One of the destructive marauding animals, the wild boar, typically weighs as much as 300 pounds (660 kg). When the boar invades the

The bluish-black tongue is what breeders prefer for their Shar-Pei puppies.

vegetable gardens and rice fields of unlucky farmers, its sharp, curved tusks can inflict serious damage on the humans or animals seeking to control them. On certain occasions, special boar hunting teams composed of crack sharpshooters and trained Shar-Pei are called for assistance.

Early Standards

Although an ancient Chinese proverb tells us, "Dogs are better than men know," breeders, judges, and owners will be quick to tell you that there is no perfect dog. The Standard outlines in precise language the characteristics of the championship-perfect dog, and thus becomes the guideline for breeding programs.

Even according to the HKKA Standard that accompanied the first dogs, however, breeders in both countries recognized that some of the Shar-Pei arriving in America were imperfect specimens. Casual crossbreeding, equally casual recordkeeping, and a diluted genetic pool had

SHAR-PEI SOUNDBITES

Two thousand years ago, the Chinese Shar-Pei, skilled at hunting mongoose, tracking wild boar, protecting livestock and guarding his master's domain, was the peasant's utility dog of choice.

resulted in a mixed bag of dogs. The coat, the tail, and, in particular, the head contained faults that were genetically undesirable. Even today these unacceptable genes reappear in some litters.

The HKKA Standard's references to fighting dogs was another source of major concern. Also of concern was the perceived necessity, at least in the beginning, to write a new American standard applicable to the characteristics of the dogs at hand.

Consequently, it became the goal of early American breeders to set a standard that would return the Shar-Pei to its original, more perfect, form. The question of what characteristics comprised that original form soon emerged.

Establishing a Standard

The HKKA listed a bluish-black tongue as standard, for instance, and a spotted "flower" tongue as a fault. Registered dogs, however, were arriving with spotted tongues, lavender tongues, and all-pink tongues, consequences of mixed breeding somewhere in their past. Consequently, although the first American standards listed "bluish-black" as the preferred color, pink or spotted (flowered) tongues were listed as "allowable."

Eventually, and confirmed again in the revised 1998 Standard, the American club listed the solid "bluish-black" tongue as preferred for all except what are referred to as the dilute colored Shar-Pei whose tongues may be solid lavender. Spotted tongues are now recognized as a major fault. More specifically, Shar-Pei with solid pink tongues are disqualified.

A second question centered around the breed's distinctive coat. In early Shar-Pei, both coat color and coat length varied significantly. The original HKKA Standard, for instance, described two acceptable coat lengths, the extremely short (horse) coat and the long (brush) coat. Both were termed "stiff as a hairbrush." In their Standard, a "flat, long, shining" coat was listed as a fault.

To the contrary, the CSPCA 1981 Standard, probably in response to the characteristics of the dogs on hand, included what it termed the "long soft" type in its list of approved coats. Eventually, however, this variance was abandoned, and today only the horse coat and the slightly longer brush coat, which is not to exceed 1-inch (2.5 cm) in length at the withers, are recognized.

One HKKA Standard that has been retained is a firm disapproval of Shar-Pei with what is termed "parti-colored" coats. The 1998 CSPCA Standard states that "only solid colors and sable are acceptable." Any shadings of color should be variations of the same body color (except in sables that have a mix of black and fawn colored hair).

Despite the breed's outstanding success in America, the Hong Kong Kennel Club (HKKC) did not recognize the Chinese Shar-Pei breed until 1989, claiming that the purebred Shar-Pei no longer existed, having been adulterated

Loose skin and a rough coat are standards for the breed.

with other breeds. Today, however, as a result of work on both sides, both the HKKC and the HKKA recognize the purebred Chinese Shar-Pei.

Shar-Pei Benchmarks

A condensed version of the 1998 AKC Breed Standard is reproduced below:

General Appearance

The Shar-Pei is an alert, compact dog of medium size and substance; square in profile; the well-proportioned head slightly, but not overly large for the body. The breed is known for its short, harsh coat, the loose skin covering the head and body, the small ears, the "hippopotamus" muzzle shape and the high set tail.

The height is 18 to 20 inches at the withers. The weight is 45 to 60 pounds.

Head and Skull

The large head has profuse wrinkles on the forehead and framing the face. The eyes are dark, small, almond-shaped and sunken. Ears, extremely small, rather thick, equilateral triangles in shape, slightly rounded at the tips.

SHAR-PEI SOUNDBITES

The Chinese language has no noun plurals, therefore there is no "s" on Shar-Pei. We refer to "three Spaniels," "four Dalmatians," and "five Shar-Pei."

The Shar-Pei's muzzle is one of the distinctive features of the breed. It is broad and full with no suggestion of snippiness. (The length from nose to stop is approximately the same as from stop to occiput.) The preferred color of the tongue is solid bluish-black. Dilute colors may have a lavender tongue. A spotted pink tongue is a major fault. A solid pink tongue is a disqualification.

Neck, Topline, Body

The neck is medium length, full and set well into the shoulders. There are moderate to heavy folds of loose skin and abundant dewlap about the neck and throat. The topline dips slightly behind the withers, rising over the short, broad loin.

The high-set tail is a characteristic feature of the Shar-Pei. A low-set tail shall be faulted. The tail is thick and round at the base, tapering to a fine point and curling over on to either side of the back. The absence of a complete tail is a disqualification.

Forequarters and Hindquarters

When viewed from the front, forelegs are straight with elbows close to the body. Feet are moderate in size, compact and firmly set, not splayed.

Hindquarters are muscular, strong, and moderately angulated. Hind dewclaws must be removed.

Coat

The extremely harsh coat is absolutely straight and off standing on the main trunk of the body. Acceptable coat lengths may range from extremely short "horse coat" up to the "brush coat," not to exceed one inch at the withers.

Color

Only solid colors and sable are acceptable. The following colors are disqualifications:
- Albino;
- Brindle, Parti-colored;
- Spotted;
- Patterned in any combination of colors.

Temperament

The Standard describes the Shar-Pei as "regal, alert, intelligent, dignified, lordly, scowling, sober, and snobbish, essentially independent and somewhat standoffish with strangers, but extreme in his devotion to his family."

The Chinese Shar-Pei Club of America (CSPCA)

The Chinese Shar-Pei Club of America (CSPCA) was founded in 1974 to record the pedigrees of the breed, to issue certificates of registration, and to protect, guide, and encourage Shar-Pei. The 10,000 member club holds specialty and sanctioned shows at locations around the United States. Each affiliate is required to hold at least one sanctioned show

A Shar-Pei's wrinkles lessen with age.

each year. Because American Kennel Club (AKC) recognition has been the goal of the CSPCA since its inception, the relationship of both organizations has been one of helpfulness and working together toward a common goal.

The CSPCA publishes a high quality bi-monthly magazine, *The Barker*. Among its other publications is an excellent and informative illustrated guide detailing the Shar-Pei Standard.

The American Kennel Club (AKC)

The American Kennel Club (AKC), founded in 1884, is a nonprofit organization comprised of almost 400 dog clubs throughout the United States. Its primary purpose is to foster and maintain interest in the health and welfare of purebred dogs.

Over 130 breeds are divided into seven major groups: Sporting, Hound, Working, Terrier, Toy, Non-Sporting, and Herding. An eighth category, Miscellaneous, is reserved for breeds recently introduced into the United States yet have "substantial, sustained, nationwide interest and activity." The Shar-Pei's acceptance into this Miscellaneous category was the first step for full recognition.

With its acceptance into the AKC as a member of the Non-Sporting group, however, the Shar-Pei joined a group that includes its Asian friend, the Chow Chow, as well as the Bichon Frise, Boston Terrier, Bulldog, Dalmatian, French Bulldog, Keeshond, Lhasa Apso, Poodle, Schipperke, Tibetan Spaniel, and Tibetan Terrier.

CSPCA Code of Ethics

The CSPCA has adopted a Code of Ethics regarding the conduct of its members. The Code, dedicated to the "care, protection and advancement" of the Shar-Pei, can serve as a standard for owners of all breeds.

Members are asked to recognize that having a dog is a lifelong commitment, whether that dog be a companion or show dog. Such canine companions should be provided clean water, quality food, exercise and veterinary care throughout their lives.

The Code is a reminder that dogs too young, too old, or too ill should not be bred. New owners should be provided with the dog's pedigree and be informed of potential health problems. Breeders should be prepared to accept dogs that are returned back to them.

Basically, the Code asks that an owner at all times "do my best for my club, my breed, and especially my dogs."

UNDERSTANDING YOUR SHAR-PEI

Perhaps more than any other breed, your Shar-Pei needs an owner who understands his history, who recognizes his intelligence, and who will appreciate his personality.

Knowledgeable owners, breeders, and judges, working together within the standard, assure sound, top-quality Shar-Pei puppies.

When you join that distinguished group, you also will be able to recognize and evaluate a Shar-Pei's hippo muzzle, meat mouth, coin tail, and flower tongue. And, what's more important, you will know how to pet a dog that has hair the consistency of sandpaper.

The breed was named for its short, stiff coat. Shar-Pei literally means sand-skin: *shar* (in Chinese, pronounced sah), and *pei* (pay) are loosely translated as rough, sandy coat. Traditionally, as well, the plural p-e-i-s is not used. You have one Shar-Pei, two Shar-Pei, forty Shar-Pei.

Take a close look at your Shar-Pei and its inherited traits.

How do you classify a breed that has captured the hearts of thousands since its arrival in the United States? The best answer, perhaps, is from one loving owner who said, "The Shar-Pei is a people dog, owned by dog people."

Look past the squirming puppy for a moment to visualize the mature, responsible dog he can become. It will be your task to assist in that transformation. As you and your puppy take those first steps to maturity, pause for a moment to contemplate your dog's heritage.

Dogs are not just furry little people. A dog's heritage is preprogrammed with set rules and behavioral regulations that cannot be overcome. And why would you want to? Why not work within those tendencies?

Canine friends are as dependent on heritage and instinct for their temperament as they are for those soulful eyes. Regardless of your feelings for what you recognize as your pet's

human characteristics, remember its heritage and don't deny it the chance to be a dog.

The Shar-Pei—
A Doll of a Dog

Using the analogy of a nested set of Russian dolls, one uniquely painted figure fits inside another. Lift one doll and another appears, each doll smaller than the last, but part of the whole. So it is with your pet. The inner, most basic figure is the dog itself. The dog has characteristics and features distinct from any other animal. Covering that dog layer are the specific tendencies of the breed. Some breeds are better hunters, herders, retrievers, than others, for instance. The final layer, the layer you see, is your own Buddy, carefully trained, socialized, and polished by you. Unique, yet a part of, and inseparable from its heritage. To help your dog develop to its highest potential, understand and work within its natural tendencies.

The trained Shar-Pei is man's protector.

Doll One—It's a Dog's World

A Shar-Pei is a member of the domestic dog family, *Canis familiaris*. The dog, like its cousins the jackal, coyote, and fox, is a close relative of *Canis lupus*, the common wolf. Unlike the wolf, the dog has been honored through recorded history as man's best friend, man's companion, and man's protector. Widely recognized for their devotion to duty, many canines have been honored for bravery in times of disaster and disorder.

Body Language

Behavioral studies of dogs have shown that all breeds exhibit similar reactions to similar situations. Knowledge of what a dog is trying to communicate with body language can be of immense help, not only to delivery people, meter readers, and census takers, but to dog owners as well. It is because of these early studies that you are cautioned to pay close attention to what your own body language is saying to your Buddy when you train, discipline, or praise him. From the very beginning, you must be sure your pet sees you as the leader in charge. You must make sure to reinforce that leadership position by handling any challenges to authority immediately and resolutely.

Dominance/Submission

The dog is a pack-oriented animal. In the pack's social hierarchy, dominant/submissive behavior is instinctive. According to pack rules, only one member can hold the position of leader. Animal behaviorists studying the wolf pack refer to this leader, usually a male, as the

Alpha wolf. The Alpha has the responsibility for settling arguments, keeping order, and giving direction to the pack members.

The Alpha transmits these instructions by certain dominant actions recognized by the other members. They, in turn, signal acceptance or defiance by their own body language. When pack discipline breaks down, the Alpha dispenses swift correction. If correction is not accepted, a battle ensues. If the challenger is successful, it assumes the position of Alpha.

A dog expressing his dominance over another dog, for instance, will stand over him, make eye contact, and growl. Occasionally, dominant males, and females too, will rest a leg on the back of the dog they are attempting to dominate, in effect, mounting him.

A dog submitting to another holds his head down, flattens his ears, and tucks his tail. He will lower his abdomen to ground level, sometimes dragging it on the ground. He will wag his hind end. If necessary, a submissive dog will lie on his back, exposing his throat. He will try to lick the aggressor. He may urinate.

A dog resisting or testing dominance will try to stand as tall as possible. He will hold his head high. His ears and tail will be erect and still. He will bark and approach the other, often standing three or four feet away. He will stare directly at the intruder.

A dog's body language also will signal a willingness to play. A dog in playful stance will lower the front part of his body and stick his rump in the air, tail wagging. He often will change position, barking at you. His front paws may make small digging motions. His eyes will be bright and alert.

Most Shar-Pei are homebodies and rarely stray.

This inherited behavior naturally carries over into human confrontations. Using the same body signals, the dog tests for dominance and either submits to or defies leadership.

The Dominant Dog and You

Encountering an aggressive dog not under control of his owner, or not under good restraint, can be a frightening experience. Dog behaviorists advise the unwary visitor challenged by an adult Alpha dog to stay calm, and to avoid any appearance of retreat. Leave the area slowly, walking sideways if possible, holding one arm out to the side as a visual distraction. Speak to the dog in a low, soothing, calming voice. Avoid direct eye contact.

Habit and Instinct

Instinctively, a mother dog finds and prepares a nest for her puppies. Reaching well back into her ancestry for maternal advice,

she is well prepared to birth and tend her litter. Those same newborn puppies, born blind and deaf, also instinctively will search out and unerringly attach themselves to her nipples within the first few minutes of birth.

Burying Bones

The habit of burying bones is a holdover from a dog's wolf past. When the wild animal hunts for his food he often covers a range of 20 miles (32 km) a day, sometimes bringing down more food than it can consume or protect. Any prey not consumed immediately or shared with the pack is fair game for other predators. The advantage of a well-concealed hiding place helps assure a meal the next day.

Circling

Because the effort to locate, kill, and transport food required a journey of several days or weeks, the hunter and his dog frequently slept in the open. The hunter gathered weeds and brush to form a bed of sorts. In search of more comfort, both members of the team stamped down and trod on the pile to soften the fibers. Today, although your pet often will flop on his stomach and go to sleep where he drops, the Shar-Pei is one of many breeds that will circle once or twice before it settles down.

Territorial Marking

The male dog's habit of urinating on posts and trees within his territory is a way of notifying other dogs that a neighborhood is occupied. Often, the passing canine stranger also will mark the tree, perhaps as a competitive signal. Note that because the dog cocks his leg, the mark is high enough to be identified, and is less likely to be erased.

SHAR-PEI SOUNDBITES

Chinese gamblers and dog-fight fanatics, seeking to improve their odds, are said to have encouraged the breeding of aggressive, loose-skinned dogs with bristly hair. The loose skin better enabled the dog to wiggle out of an attack, and the hair was distasteful in an adversary's mouth.

Denning

The dog, in addition to being a pack animal, has a strong denning instinct. Watch your dog as he selects a location for a nap. He will opt for the security of a spot under the kitchen table, behind an easy chair, or along a wall. He will not turn his back on the entrance, but rather will set his face toward the activity center of the room.

The instinctive denning preference is important to the concept of crate training discussed in Housetraining Your Puppy (see page 38).

Doll Two—The Shar-Pei as a Breed

Covering the inner dog is the second layer in our wooden nest, the breed layer. This layer contains additional instinctive and hereditary traits unique to the Shar-Pei.

Today's Shar-Pei is a survivor. His ancestors were farm dogs and fighting dogs. They were guardians of the home and income producers as well. Those dogs who survived this often harsh environment were strong, intelligent, and loyal.

*Toys are essentials
for the Shar-Pei puppy.*

External Appearance

Your Shar-Pei should be a stocky, compact dog, alert and ready to work or play. His eyes should not have needed tacking (page 85), nor his coat trimming.

When full grown, the Chinese Shar-Pei, a medium-sized dog, will weigh 40 to 55 pounds (18–25 kg). His adult height will be approximately 18 to 20 inches (46–51 cm) at the withers. (The dog's withers are between and slightly higher than the shoulder blades.)

Coat: The harsh coat is one of the breed's most distinguishing features. Two lengths are acceptable. The shortest coat, less than ½ inch (1.3 cm), is called the horse coat. (In China, the native horses have bristly, as opposed to silky, coats. The hair stands out at an 8 degree angle.) Some judges and breeders are of the opinion that the number of horse coats being shown has decreased in recent years.

The slightly longer brush coat is identified as having hair longer than ½ inch (1.3 cm), but under no circumstances longer than 1 inch (2.5 cm) at the withers. The Shar-Pei has no undercoat.

The coat is separated into two color types: basic and dilute. Basic colors, which can include some shading along the back and ears of the dog, include cream (off-white), all shades of brown (fawn, red, brown, sable), silver, and black.

The dilute colored Shar-Pei (cream, apricot, five-point-red, sable, chocolate, and silver) are of a uniform color with no shading.

The tongue, eyes, nose, and nails of a basic colored Shar-Pei are black. The dilute colors may have a lavender tongue, self-colored skin, nose, and nails, and amber eyes.

Distinctive Features

The muzzle of the Shar-Pei is broad and usually well-padded. The typical shape gave the dog his hippopotamus-muzzle nickname. Two types of muzzle are evident: a dog is referred to as a meat-mouth if its muzzle is heavily padded.

Those Shar-Pei with less mouth padding are called bone-mouths. Under no circumstances is there a suggestion of snipiness in the bone-mouth muzzle.

There seems to be a general preference for the meat-mouth look, because the shape of the muzzle has broadened in recent years. Be aware that heavily padded muzzles can contribute to breathing difficulties, snoring, slobbering, and bad tooth alignment.

The eyes of a Shar-Pei are small, almond-shaped, and sunken. The triangular shaped ears

Keep training sessions short to maintain your puppy's attention.

are extremely small. The ears lie flat against the head and point toward the eyes.

The typical Shar-Pei tail is high set, and carried high. The reasoning behind the preference for a high tailset is that a cowardly dog tucks his tail between his legs, and the Shar-Pei is no coward. It is a matter of personal preference if a dog's tail curls over its back or is straight. Some lines carry a curly, "coin" tail gene that is in much demand.

The excessive puppy wrinkles that have charmed so many usually disappear by adulthood. Most mature Shar-Pei, although almost always loose-skinned, retain only head, neck, and withers wrinkling.

Temperament and Behavior

These "funny, wrinkled little dogs" don't come with a book of instructions. But if they did, one of the first would be a reminder to take the time to appreciate the Shar-Pei's unique temperament. That adorable, cuddly puppy will grow into a strong, opinionated, adult dog.

The Chinese Shar-Pei, an intelligent, loyal worker, is happiest when he feels useful. In his own mind, he already has defined his proper socially useful role. Historically a guard dog, the Shar-Pei has an inborn tendency to protect his home and human pack. He will extend great loyalty and affection to his family. Unless properly and carefully socialized, however, he

This puppy still has some growing to do.

often will refuse to extend that affection to others and can be aggressive to other animals as well as to strangers.

Today's Shar-Pei is not a barker, but he will bark when threatened. He is a good watchdog, but he does not overreact. He is not a fighting dog, but he can be made to fight. If the instincts of generations of fighting dogs surface, he will defend himself and his family.

The Shar-Pei is an instinctively clean dog that rarely sheds. He requires no special clipping or grooming. He is easily housetrained.

Most Shar-Pei are homebodies and rarely stray. Owners usually say that their dogs prefer the company of humans, although they also enjoy the company of other family dogs, particularly other Shar-Pei.

Most Shar-Pei will accept children as members of the family, but most adult Shar-Pei will not tolerate for long the teasing and abuse of a young child. On the other hand, the dog could assume an overly possessive behavior toward the child, to the point of standing between the child and the parents. Introduce your pet and your children slowly and sensibly.

Breed Hardiness

Hereditary problems in the Chinese Shar-Pei are concentrated in three major areas: eyes, skin, and internal. Because of the limited gene pool available to United States breeders, these and other genetic problems filtered into many Shar-Pei lines. Today, each of these inherited inclinations is the subject of intensive study.

Furthermore, responsible breeders remove puppies identified with such tendencies from the breeding system. Nevertheless, be aware that many outwardly charming but genetically defective Shar-Pei are still being bred by incautious owners. These dogs and their unfortunate descendants are on the market today.

Eye problems: Entropion is a genetic eye problem that causes the puppy's eyelids to roll inward. As a result, the eyelashes rubbing against the cornea cause acute distress for the victim. Entropion, induced in part by the excessive folds of skin around his face, can involve one or both eyes, and either upper or lower lid.

Although the condition can appear at birth, indeed, can develop before the puppy's eyes even open, symptoms usually are observed at about four weeks. Early symptoms of eye problems include pawing at the eyes and tearing.

SHAR-PEI SOUNDBITES

Farmers near the South China Sea depended on the breed's famous "Warrior Scowl" and menacing appearance to help repel barbarian raiders.

Treatment of severe, adult entropion calls for surgical removal of a part of the affected eyelid. Responsible owners will not breed a dog that required adult entropion surgery.

Skin problems: The Shar-Pei, because of his unusually sensitive skin, is considered an allergy-prone breed. Allergic reactions, caused by food or by the environment, range from reddened skin to hair loss to the itching and oozing sores produced by constant scratching.

The inhalant allergies most recognized in Shar-Pei include tree and grass pollens, molds, and house dust. One offending food source frequently cited by owners is the soybean.

Because sensitivity is hereditary, some lines exhibit greater allergic tendencies than others.

Further discussion of allergies, sensitivities, and treatments can be found in the Shar-Pei Health Care chapter.

Internal problems: An imbalance in the immune system of some Shar-Pei results in an increased susceptibility to some diseases. Upper respiratory infections, inner ear problems, and gastrointestinal upsets are typical manifestations.

Some Shar-Pei lines carry a tendency to a thyroid deficiency that results in skin problems. Known as hypothyroidism, this endocrine disorder can cause hair loss, dry skin, and fluid buildup, particularly on the legs.

The condition usually doesn't manifest itself until age four to six, considered middle age in Shar-Pei. Early observable symptoms include weight gain and lethargy.

Hypothyroidism is treatable. With careful management and hormone replacement therapy, the dog will regain its former vitality and resume an active, normal life.

Doll Three—Your Own Buddy

The final, most visible layer in our nest of dolls is the personality and being of your own Shar-Pei.

Ideally, your own Buddy will be well-socialized. He will love you, follow you, obey you. When playing, he will recognize his strength. Although somewhat aloof with strangers, he will not be aggressive to the veterinarian or to other adults and children who have been properly introduced.

A big muzzle and lots of wrinkles give the Shar-Pei its distinctive appearance.

A sandpaper-like coat is part and parcel of a healthy Shar-Pei.

How can you be sure your adorable Bud will still be adorable when he weighs 50 pounds (23 kg)? Puppies are cute. People tend to forgive their indiscretions. Indiscreet grown dogs are not cute. At the very least, an untrained adult dog is a nuisance. A well-behaved pet earns a place in everyone's affection when its obedience is routine behavior. Obedience becomes routine as a consequence of discipline and training.

According to the Morris Animal Foundation, most of the lists naming the leading causes of death in dogs ignore the number one cause: euthanasia for behavior. The Foundation cites behavioral problems as the reason millions of family pets are taken to animal shelters each year. Many of these dogs are poorly trained adolescent/puppies that turned, in self-defense, to aggression and disobedience.

Shar-Pei and Public Perception

Perhaps because of the breed's perpetual frown, its fearsome growl, or its overstated reputation for fighting, the adult Shar-Pei often is viewed by the public as a fearsome dog. Will the "pit bull" ordinances one day come to sit on the Shar-Pei's doorstep also? Although many of these ordinances are not "breed specific," meaning not mentioned by name, letters to the editor call for bans on Rottweilers, Chow Chows, and others known as guard dogs.

It is up to dog owners to police their breed. Dogs should be kept under control at all times, their socialization training should begin at a very young age, and owners should be alert to the rumblings in their own communities.

JOINING THE FAMILY

A Shar-Pei puppy parades around the house wearing her grandfather's pajamas. Helping your charming Princess develop into her full potential, including filling those baggy pants, is an experience you will treasure forever.

What to Look For in a Shar-Pei Puppy

Because the Shar-Pei is known as a "head" breed, first examine that profusely wrinkled face. At eight weeks of age the traditional Shar-Pei scowl more closely resembles that of a frowning baby than that of a fierce fighting dog. Touch her muzzle. American breeders compare the perfect Shar-Pei muzzle to the muzzle of a well-padded hippopotamus. Chinese breeders see a resemblance to the more ascetic shape of an Oriental roof tile.

Look at the puppy's bite. The perfect bite is a scissors bite in which the upper front teeth fit over the lower.

The puppy's tongue and mouth should be bluish-black unless the puppy's coloring is one of the six dilute colors, in which case the puppy will have no black pigmentation anywhere. If the puppy is a dilute, the color of her tongue will vary from light to dark lavender.

The puppy's ears should be triangular and very small, lying flat against the puppy's head. Prick ears are a disqualification. An earlier standard compared the perfect ear size to that of a human thumbnail. Today, just enough flap to cover the ear opening is considered sufficient.

Take a good look at the puppy's eyes. Look for signs of puppy eye tacking. Remember that many breeders offer Shar-Pei litters in which none of the puppies or their parents required eye tacks.

Reach out and touch that velvet-appearing fur. Surprisingly harsh, isn't it? That short, stiff coat is one of the distinguishing features of your new friend. A healthy Shar-Pei coat never exceeds 1 inch (2.5 cm) in length and usually sticks absolutely straight out.

Are you ready to share your life with a Shar-Pei puppy?

Do you want a show dog or a pet?

Show Dog or Pet?

Although the perfect Shar-Pei has yet to be born, new puppies are always graded against the standard of perfection. Some breeders can spot a potential show dog right away. Others check the puppy over a period of several months before making a firm statement.

A dog with show potential will cost more initially. You might have to spend at least one night in another city, or pay shipping charges. If you look forward to a show career for your Shar-Pei, buy the best dog you can afford from a breeder you like and trust.

Most owners have no intention of showing their dogs. They are going to be very happy with a healthy, well-trained, pet Shar-Pei. You may be sure that responsible breeders give pet-quality dogs the same care, vaccinations, and deworming as those destined for show homes.

Male or Female?

There is a size difference in male and female adult Shar-Pei. The males, as a rule, are taller and heavier than the females. If you are looking for a house pet and have no interest in breeding, your prime considerations could be that the female, unless spayed, will have to be given special care twice a year during her estrus (heat) periods. The adult male, unless neutered, usually has a greater tendency to roam.

Puppy or Grown Dog?

The knowledge that a young life depends upon you for its very existence can be a satisfying challenge. That's one reason many people choose to begin with a youngster.

Sometimes, though, a wonderful, loving adult dog is returned to the breeder or even brought to the Humane Society through no fault of her own. Maybe her family moved into an apartment that didn't allow pets. Perhaps someone in the human family developed an allergy. Such rescued older dogs are often perfect pets for a family that wants love, affection, and amusement.

An adult Shar-Pei can be less work for everyone. An adult normally doesn't require housebreaking, is usually past the chewing stage, and is trained not to bark or get on furniture.

What Age Puppy Is Best?

Veterinarian behaviorists tell us not to remove a puppy from the litter until she can eat and thrive physically and emotionally away from her mother and littermates. For most puppies, that date is around eight to nine weeks of age.

Where to Purchase Your Shar-Pei

There are many sources for purebred dogs. Kennels advertise in national magazines. Home breeders post signs in veterinarians' offices. Appealing puppies frolic in pet stores.

First, ask your veterinarian for advice. Ask about local dealers and breeders. Your veterinarian will be familiar with lines free of congenital problems, and will guide you toward those sources.

Contact a local dog fanciers group. Attend a dog show.

Questions You Might Ask or Be Asked

Breeders will tell you that no one dog is right for every person's needs. Much depends on your own personality, the amount of space you have available, and the amount of time you can devote to training. Shar-Pei breeders work hard to place their puppies with caring and understanding dog lovers who see the understuffed pups as something other than a casual fancy. Indeed, most breeders follow strict guidelines when sizing up potential owners.

Most, for example, will refuse to sell two puppies to the same family at the same time. The theory is, first, that each puppy should receive special attention. Second, the bond is stronger when the puppy focuses solely on you without the added distraction of a littermate.

They may ask if you have previously owned a dog, and if so, what happened to her. They may ask about already existing household pets.

Knowing that the Shar-Pei's natural instincts are alert and ever ready, a breeder will warn you that the breed's hunter heritage can bring out aggression toward pet rabbits, hamsters, and white mice, for instance.

You may be asked about family allergies. The stiff Shar-Pei coat can cause an itchy, irritable skin rash on susceptible persons. Not every coat causes this rash. Nor does everyone who comes in contact with a particular Shar-Pei develop the rash. Nevertheless, the reaction is common enough that the condition is known as Shar-Pei rash.

You may be asked if someone will be at home all day with the puppy or if she will spend the day alone. A puppy must learn to be alone, must learn to amuse itself, to sleep, eat, and play without the company of people or of other dogs. However, the Shar-Pei is a sociable animal and will be unhappy if left alone for any length of time without you or at least another pet for company.

The first few days can be lonesome.

Most breeders will want to know if you have children. They will want to know if any of the children are under age six. If you do have children under age six, you might be asked to leave the puppy at the kennel until she is at least nine to twelve weeks old. Because behaviorists have proven that it is important for the puppy to make human friends early, your breeder will see to it that the belated adoptee receives the socialization she requires.

As for your own questions, inquire about the puppy's pedigree. Ask about its strengths and weaknesses. Ask to see the puppy's parents. A kennel will, at the very least, have photographs of the sire and dam. Are the quarters clean? Are there any puppies with runny noses? Diarrhea? Do the owners seem knowledgeable?

Many otherwise beautiful puppies are prone to allergies. Ask about skin problems. Ask if the puppy's parents had any problems with itching, eczema, or dermatitis.

Inquire about hip dysplasia. Canine hip dysplasia is an inherited problem. Have the parents been X-rayed? Have the X-rays been sent to the Orthopedic Foundation for Animals (OFA) for evaluation?

Inquire about the health history of both lines. Ask about entropion. Did either of the parents require puppy eye tacking or perhaps adult eye surgery?

Responses to these and similar questions will help you make your selection. No thoughtful dealer or breeder will object to answering them honestly.

Some breeders will give you a written guarantee against hereditary diseases. Most will assume basic responsibility for the puppy up to a week after purchase. This could include assuming some portion of the medical expenses. It also could include replacing a sick puppy with a healthy one. If you are not offered this choice, you should ask. If you are refused, you have a right to take your business elsewhere.

Costs

Owning any dog can be expensive. The initial purchase price of a show-quality Shar-Pei can be several thousand dollars. In addition to the purchase price, you should be prepared to finance 10 to 13 years of health care, shelter, proper food, and training. When estimating expenses, keep in mind the possibility of such unexpected expenditures as repair of congenital problems, pregnancy, or accident.

Pet Personality Test

Behavior testing has long been a part of a dog owner's skills. In the past, it was imperative that the farmer or herdsman select the most apt of the litters to train as replacement workers. A form of behavior testing was also an extremely important part of selective breeding. When only the best of a litter were given food and shelter, the substandard members of the breed automatically were weeded out.

Many modern dog behaviorists have contributed greatly to our knowledge of dogs and their world. Clarence Pfaffenberger, in his work with Guide Dogs for the Blind, was instrumental in developing early testing of potential candidates.

In 1975, William E. Campbell, a canine behaviorist and regular contributor to *Modern Veterinary Practice* magazine, developed a very practical Puppy Behavior Selection Test designed to fit puppies to people. The test focuses on the puppy's attraction to humans, its

All puppies need plenty of exercise and lots of rest.

leadership potential, and its tendencies to physical or social dominance. Properly administered, a testing program such as this can point out the potential bully as well as the puppy with a gentler nature. The entire test can be run on a full litter in less than an hour, which is little enough time to select a lifelong companion.

Before you run any behavior tests, however, take stock of your own needs. Keep in mind the type of mature dog you want. If you are looking for a show dog, you might want to select a puppy that steps out confidently, one that would enjoy the travel, the hustle, and long hours of the show ring, one not afraid of strange sights and sounds. On the other hand, if your idea of a night out is a slow walk around the block and then home, a puppy with a lower energy level might be the one you would want.

Perhaps, though, you won't need to test the entire litter. Your choice may be limited to only one or two puppies. Keeping in mind the type of mature dog you want, test these two puppies. Focus on your concept of the ideal companion dog for your lifestyle.

Although not as comprehensive as the original test program, the following situations have been adapted from these and other standard tests. Following this simple procedure will help you to make a judgment on each puppy.

With paper and pencil at hand, observe each puppy as it interacts with others. Make a note of that puppy's reactions to the breeder, to its dam, and to other members of the litter. Then carry each puppy, one at a time, into a quiet area, one free of distractions. Set the puppy down.

Social or Antisocial?

Step away from the puppy and try to attract her to you. Use whatever means you can, short of touching the puppy, to gain her attention and interest. Speak in a low voice, whistle, pat the ground. See how willingly the puppy comes, how quickly she comes, or whether she comes at all. A shy puppy will be the one hardest to attract. A highly sociable puppy literally will follow you home.

Curious or Indifferent?

Stand next to the puppy. Now turn and walk in the opposite direction. (Be sure the puppy is aware that you walked away.) Some puppies will follow immediately, others will race ahead of you. Some will ignore you. Whether the puppy follows you, stays still, or walks the other way can be a test of her interest in you.

Submissive or Dominant?

Gently roll the puppy onto her back. With one hand on her chest, hold her down for about 30 seconds. How does the puppy respond? Does she object? If so, how long does she take to settle down? Some puppies wiggle and squirm at first and then lie quietly. Other puppies object strongly to such behavior, setting up a loud racket, struggling, and nipping at your fingers. Which type of dog do you prefer?

Your puppy's personality should be compatible with yours.

Calm or Hyper?

Can you calm the puppy? Gently stroke the puppy's back, from head to tail. Do this several times until you get a clear reaction. Some puppies will accept your dominance. Some will try to escape. Others will bite or growl. What kind of reaction did you obtain? How long did the puppy take to react?

Adaptable or Unmanageable?

This last test is similar to the previous test, except that this time the puppy has no control over the situation. You are in total control. Put both hands around the puppy's belly, and lift her off the ground to waist level. How permissive is the puppy to this situation? How much does she struggle, and for how long? Those puppies who struggle very little will be easy to manage. Those puppies who are very upset and aggressively try to escape will need a firmer hand.

The Results

Evaluate the results in the light of your own observations of the litter. Talk to the breeder about the results of the testing. Listen to the breeder's recommendations. Take your time. Use your own judgment. In the end, select the puppy that appeals to you, that best suits your own lifestyle, and that seems to beg, "Take me home, please."

Before You Bring Your Puppy Home

First, let me congratulate you! Your new Chinese Shar-Pei puppy is destined to evolve into a highly intelligent, instinctively loyal companion that will be a joy to own. I know that you spent hours making the decision to bring this squirmy, bristly puppy into your life. You willingly accepted the responsibility to care for another living being. You no doubt have invested a considerable amount of money already, and accept the fact that future expenditures are on the way. You're both very lucky. You are taking the first steps on the journey to a long and enviable relationship. Congratulations!

Supply Checklist

Now that the puppy is eight weeks old, Princess is ready to leave the litter. Have you selected a special place to feed her? A special spot for elimination? Where will the puppy sleep? Will she have a bed of her very own? The first few days will be smoother if you have a few items already on hand for when the puppy arrives.

Your puppy's want list is short and simple. She will need love and affection and a few basic supplies to call her own. When the puppy arrives at your home, she would appreciate:
- ✔ a food dish
- ✔ a water bowl
- ✔ a bed
- ✔ a chew toy

I am sure that later you will expand this list to include a collar and lead, balls, grooming utensils, shampoos, brushes, more toys, and so on. The list is endless.

Your Puppy and the Veterinarian

An early relationship with a nearby veterinarian is an important part of being a responsible dog owner. You should take your puppy to a veterinarian for a well-puppy checkup. Then, when you need veterinary services later, your

For a healthy puppy, bonding is a must with a human family.

veterinarian will have a baseline upon which to make decisions.

Not only will your veterinarian suggest ways to reduce your initial expenses, many will offer advice on diet, supplements, and ongoing care. You will be instructed on procedures you can do at home, such as deworming, to reduce the need for successive office visits. In addition, your veterinarian can provide you with free brochures designed to take the mystery out of animal health care.

Try to select a veterinarian near your neighborhood. In an emergency, travel time is very important. Talk to your neighbors. Check with your local breed club, if one is available. Ask members of the local kennel club for recommendations. Get recommendations from the knowledgeable staff at the Humane Society.

Then, walk up to the office door and go in. Talk to the staff. Are they professional looking and acting? Are they friendly? Ask to look at the kennels. Are they clean? Ask about fees. Are they reasonable?

Once you have selected your veterinarian, a special relationship is born. Your veterinarian will be your and your dog's best friend.

Naming Your Puppy

Your puppy's name should not duplicate the name of any other Shar-Pei, living or dead. Although you may believe that all the best names have been used, don't sell your own ingenuity short. Adapt or twist these names into something uniquely yours.

The best advice is to keep the call name simple. You may select an Asian name translated into English, an English phrase translated into Chinese, an English name with an Asian flair, or whatever you like. We named our charmer Shar-Ming Buhd-Dee, and call him Buddy.

A glance at a show catalog will reveal Ah Choo, Sir Choo, Foo Man Choo, Chop Sooy, and Chu'd Slipper. Au Ghee, Au Sum, and Dem Sum Wrinkles are friends of ours. So are Ro-Z, Foo-Z, and Soo-Z-Q.

How to Treat Your Puppy

Now, what plans do you have for your life together? Your responsibility now is to decide exactly how you want this new relationship to progress. If you have decided that you will be the dominant member in this pack, and that Princess will be a follower, you must be very clear in relaying this to the puppy. If you watch television, the puppy will want to settle down on the

sofa beside you. Will you permit this? If you open the car door, your new friend will want to jump in the front seat with you. Is this seating arrangement your idea or the puppy's? When you leave your new puppy alone, she will let you know she feels abandoned. Can you cope?

These are the natural reactions of a puppy that has bonded to its master. The puppy's second natural reaction is that she will be aware of your moods and will be very sensitive to them. She will want to please you in order to be happy in her new home.

Use the puppy's desire to bond, and her clear desire to please you as tools in your training repertoire. Set the limits, and, one by one, introduce Princess to the rules of behavior in her new life.

The guidelines in this book are distilled from the experiences of many successful dog trainers and behaviorists. The first statement each of those trainers would make is that, even in purebred dogs, each one is an individual. So, the first guideline is know your dog. Watch the puppy when you talk to her and work with her. If she doesn't follow through on a procedure, she probably doesn't understand what you want of her. Pay attention to what the puppy is telling you in terms of attitude and response time. Then work within the puppy's own temperament to achieve the results you want.

Lifting

Older children, and even adults, need to be taught how to lift a puppy without injuring her. Never let anyone pick up the puppy by the scruff of the neck or with one hand under the abdomen. Watch newcomers around your puppy. The puppy will bound forward and jump up, begging to be lifted. If the newcomer leans

Your puppy's parents will tell you a lot about your new pet.

forward and tries to lift the puppy by her front legs, step in immediately.

Demonstrate to your visitor how to use both hands to lift a puppy. One hand should be placed firmly under the puppy's chest. The second hand should support its heavy little rump.

Children are especially drawn to puppies. In the child's attempts to cuddle a squirming 15-pound (7-kg) baby animal, the puppy often lands headfirst on the floor. She picks herself up and runs off yelping. After being disciplined, the child feels guilty and, promising to be careful, goes off in search of the puppy again. The puppy, wanting nothing more to do with such turmoil, hides under a chair.

Avoid that scene. Be firm about not letting young children pick up the puppy. Insist instead that very young children sit down when playing with the puppy. Sit beside them. Encourage the child to stroke the puppy's back and head.

Tone of Voice

Trainers often single out two important rules for talking to dogs. One is to be consistent in your choice of words. Most trainers tell us that dogs have a limited understanding of language. If you want your puppy to stop doing something, for instance, don't confuse the puppy. If on one occasion you say, "stop that," and on another occasion say, "Princess, quit it," the message you send will not be as clear as "no." A simple "no" in a firm, authoritative tone of voice is best every time.

The second rule to remember is to use a decidedly different tone of voice for praise and for correction. Even an untrained dog can understand the vocal implications of your message. It is your tone of voice, in conjunction with the words you use, that is of primary importance.

Be sure your praise voice is markedly different from your disciplinary voice. Cultivate a happy, singing tone to praise the puppy.

Have food, water, and treats on hand before the puppy arrives.

Raise your pitch, put a lilt in your voice. Make it known that you think your puppy is the brightest, best doggy in the world. "What a good dog!" chanted by a loving voice is music to a puppy's ears.

The Right Toys

Don't give the puppy lightweight plastic to chew. Any self-respecting Shar-Pei will demolish such a toy within an hour and could swallow and subsequently choke on the pieces. Also avoid those "squeak" toys with whistles or noisemakers that might break off and be swallowed. At the very least, remember to remove the whistle and to inspect the toy frequently. If a toy seems too cute to pass up, allow the puppy to play with some of the sturdier ones under close supervision by you. When the toy shows signs of wear, replace it.

Our puppies loved an old white cotton sock that had been knotted around a canning jar ring. The ring served as an easy-to-carry handle. The metal produced a satisfactory noise when the toy was dragged across the floor.

Although puppies love the smell of you, and would adore to chew on an old shoe, giving in to this urge is not a good idea. It's always best not to put temptation in the puppy's way. The puppy won't be able to tell the difference between her old shoe and your new tennis shoes. Someday that distinction will be very important.

Veterinarians recommend giving your pet natural bones that have been processed, or bones made of hard plastic or nylon. Be cautious in giving extremely hard bones to puppies. Some of these products are so hard that puppies' teeth have been chipped.

Take your time and talk to the breeder when choosing your puppy.

The first rule in training puppies is that there are no rules. No two puppies learn the same way. Just remember: try not to let your Shar-Pei puppy engage in any errant behavior, however cute, that would be unacceptable in adulthood.

First Lessons

By the time you bring your Buddy home, he probably will be eight or nine weeks old. Within days, the two of you already will be well on your way to that special friendship. Use these early months of puppyhood to teach relationships, loyalty, house manners, and doggy etiquette. Don't let your puppy engage in any behavior that would be unacceptable in an adult of the breed.

First of all, teach the puppy his name. Don't call "Puppy, puppy, puppy," like the breeder did in the kennel. Everybody came to that one. Use your puppy's name often. Say "Buddy, come!" and "What a good boy Buddy is!"

Teach your puppy the meaning of "no." Enforce the word by using an authoritative

Don't overwhelm your puppy on the first day in his new home.

tone of voice, a pointed finger, or a loud hand clap. The puppy will learn soon enough that "no" with or without the hand signals and noise means "stop it." Stop barking, stop getting on the sofa, stop chewing up the newspaper, just stop doing whatever it is you're doing.

Serious obedience training, usually thought of as "sit," "come," "heel," "stay," and "down," can't be started until the puppy has some self-control, usually around seven months.

Teach your puppy that you are the boss. Teach your puppy to accept attention from others, but teach him to look to you for affection, discipline, and food. Remember, the puppy is looking for a pack leader and is perfectly willing to take on the job if no one else wants it. To permit a member of a dominant breed such as the Shar-Pei to assume the role of leader of the pack is a major mistake.

Begin to assert your own dominance early by being very sure the puppy obeys you. If you don't want the puppy on the sofa, for instance, say "No!" or "Off!" (anything but "down." Save "down" for "lie down.") and be sure the puppy does as you say, no matter how cute he looks. Be very firm. Buddy must understand that either he jumps off the sofa immediately or you will lift him off. Either way, your order must be obeyed.

Don't forget the final first lesson. Praise your puppy whenever he does something right. Even if you have to push the puppy off the sofa, praise him. Use your most loving, affectionate voice. From the puppy's point of view, the praise is well-deserved.

How Soon Can You Begin?

Richard Wolters, a professional trainer, relates that you will know the exact day your puppy is ready for that first lesson. That will be the day the puppy responds to his name.

When the puppy is about eight weeks old, you might try the Wolters test. Choose a time when the puppy is lying quietly but paying no attention to you. Call the puppy by name. If the puppy keeps on chewing or scratching or whatever, and does not look up, let him be.

Try again the next day. Call the puppy by name. The first time the puppy stops and looks up at you as if to say, "Yes?" your puppy should be ready to listen to training instructions. As Wolters says, "When this happens, at that moment, (the puppy is) ready to accept his first training . . . and the results will be spectacular."

How Puppies Learn

A dog has an instinctual need to lead or be led. Once the two of you agree that you will be the leader of the pack, a certain orderliness takes place in your relationship.

Always remember that a Shar-Pei has a sensitive nature. Harsh training methods won't work. You will find that the more positive your training, and the less often you have to correct your puppy, the quicker the learning will proceed. Train your puppy fairly and use a lot of praise.

The problem may be that your puppy doesn't understand what you want. Maybe this new game is boring and tiring to your puppy, or your puppy isn't paying attention. If you give a command that is not obeyed, he may try to lick your face instead. Take some time off before you try again. But do try again. You will find that if you praise the puppy for success, however small, the puppy will do everything possible to please you.

Remember one final guideline: don't correct a puppy "after the fact." Let's say you come home one afternoon and find that your puppy has been at war with a sofa pillow. Because a dog most often associates one event with the action that precedes it, it is difficult for you to discipline the puppy for chewing on the pillow. You certainly can try. You can take the puppy to the pillow if you want to and shout at him. You can hit the puppy with the pillow. You can hold the pillow up to his nose and fuss and make a lot of noise. All that will happen is that the puppy will slink away from you. You will have made your puppy miserable. But don't think you have taught the puppy not to chew the pillow. What your puppy learned was that sometimes when you come home you are a grouch.

The First Day

Your puppy will be hungry upon arriving at his new home. Most kennel owners don't feed

Puppies are a lot of work—but they're worth it.

a puppy just before his first trip. This is probably a good idea. A carsick puppy takes a long
time to get over his distrust of cars. Consequently, if you and your puppy come home in
the middle of the afternoon, he will be tired,
confused, hungry and will need to go to the
bathroom.

Put the puppy down in the yard on the
special spot you chose ahead of time. Speak
in a low, friendly voice. Because the ride
home may have been an exhausting and perhaps frightening experience, the puppy will
probably eliminate at once. Praise the puppy
generously.

Then, if your Shar-Pei will be a house dog,
open the door and welcome your puppy home.
Let the puppy wander around a bit. Get the
puppy used to the sounds and smells of his
new family. Not too many sounds, though. Is
the noise level too high? It would be better if
the puppy could have some time to get used to
his new surroundings without being held too
much.

Try to get the puppy to lie down. If your
puppy settles down to sleep, then you've both
taken the first step toward accepting each
other as best friends.

Handling the First Night

A lonesome puppy can keep the entire house
on edge. Eventually, someone will offer to
bring the puppy into the bedroom, a solution
that works for a while because the puppy will
eventually fall asleep. Everyone in the house
smiles in relief. But when the puppy wakes up
and looks around, his lonesome wail fills the
room. Quiet is achieved only when someone
lifts the puppy onto the bed.

If this is the solution you want, it's your
house and your bed. Not quite all yours,
though. One day that puppy will weigh a hefty
50 pounds. If you prefer to have your puppy
sleep in a dog bed in his own room, you might
want to begin training early. After you have
settled the puppy into the crate, try not to

return the first time or two the puppy wails. Give the puppy a chance to settle down. Then be very matter-of-fact about leaving.

If the puppy insists that you return, go back and pet him. Stay until the puppy is calm then leave again and close the door. The puppy must get the idea that this is where he stays.

Some owners wrap a soft towel around a ticking clock or a filled hot water bottle and then place the towel in the puppy's bed. Another tunes a radio to a classical station and leaves it on overnight. Others, having done all they can, just cover their ears, snuggle into their pillows, and try to sleep knowing the puppy left an early wake-up call for tomorrow. The bladder of an eight-week-old puppy will nudge him awake early—very early—the next morning.

Housetraining Your Puppy

Housetraining an indoor puppy can be a time-consuming and frustrating chore. Often, the puppy must be trained to paper. Ultimately, when he is a little older and its bladder matures, or when the weather clears, the puppy must be convinced to go outside.

Crate training, coupled with some paper training if necessary, is not simply a method of housetraining, but is a way of life for you and your pet. For many owners who have tried both ways, crate training is the prime method of choice.

Paper Training

A puppy can be trained to eliminate in the same approximate place each time. First, if yours will be a house dog, select two special spots for the puppy's use, one inside and one outside the house. Keeping in mind that Buddy

will not soil his own den unless forced to do so, do not select an inside spot near the dog's bed or food bowls. After you have made your decision, your next problem will be convincing your little friend to agree with you.

You can help assure this agreement by sponging up a little of the puppy's urine with a sheet of newspaper. Spread this "scented" paper on top of three or four clean, double-page sheets of paper. Bring the puppy to the scented paper each time you think the need should arise.

Be alert during these two or three weeks. Be especially aware during the critical moments shortly after meals and when the puppy wakes up. Normally, a puppy will urinate after every meal, every nap, and every play session. If the puppy shows any signs of wanting to eliminate (sniffing along the floor, walking in circles, dribbling), pick up your pet immediately and carry him either to the paper or outside.

When the puppy relieves himself on the paper, praise him. Then remove the top, wettest sheet and dispose of it. Leave one slightly damp sheet as a new top. Put fresh newspaper on the bottom. Every time you clean up, leave one paper with his own damp scent on top of the pile. Soon the puppy will head for the scented paper of his own accord. Within a week, barring accidents, your puppy will be "double-page paper-trained." (You can still expect to find accidents until the puppy matures completely.)

Sometime between three and four months of age, you will want to transfer your paper-trained puppy to the outside. This should not be a big problem. The puppy will have a better understanding of your expectations, and you can take advantage of inside training habits.

Always supervise your puppy,
especially outdoors.

Pick up a sheet of the puppy's wet paper. Take the sheet outside and place it at the location you chose. Lead the puppy to the spot. This transferal is learned easily. Within a day or two you shouldn't have to bring the paper outside anymore.

Crate Training

Crate training, although the most efficient method of housetraining, is initially more time-consuming for the owner. The point of the training is that once inside the crate, Buddy will do his best to wait for you to come. Even a six- or seven-week-old puppy will bark and whine for you to let him out if you don't get back soon enough.

Understanding the denning instinct: Although crate training is the easiest, fastest way to housetrain a puppy, some people object to crating. They picture their puppy in a cage because they project their own human feelings onto a pet. Such well-meaning owners usually think of zoos and circuses where cages are used primarily for animal restraint.

Look at the crate from the dog's point of view for a minute. A dog is a den animal. Because a dog's primitive instincts are strong, these instincts control many of your pet's modern habits. Your puppy will prefer the security of a den. Today's crate provides indoor dogs with that security.

Hints on selecting a crate: Crates, usually made either of metal or fiberglass, are available at pet supply stores and from catalogs. Many crates are collapsible and thus portable.

Unless you want to buy another in four months, the crate should be large enough for a grown Shar-Pei to stand up in. An adult Shar-Pei is 18 to 20 inches (46–51 cm) high at the shoulders and holds its large head erect. This means that for comfort your dog would need a crate about 36-inches (91-cm) long and at least 30-inches (76-cm) high. This gives the dog room to turn around, change his position, and stretch out.

A second advantage of crate training is that the crate serves as a doggy den, as a traveling bed, and as a transporter on those veterinarian visits or day trips.

There are two ways to crate train. Both are for "house puppies." Either, in my opinion, is better and easier and surer than paper training. The crate should contain nothing but a washable mat for the puppy to lie down on, and perhaps a chew toy. No food or water.

The first technique is designed for use by those owners who will be at home with the puppy for most of the first two weeks. The second is for those who must train a puppy that will be left alone all day.

Puppies love to play.

(1) Try to select a location along a wall or in a corner where the puppy can see and hear the activity of the house, but is out of the mainstream of traffic. Put the puppy in the crate. Go about your business. Talk to the puppy while you work, but don't hover over the crate. Leave the puppy in the crate no longer than ten minutes. Then pick him up and play with him, cuddle him, feed him, or whatever you wish, and then put him back in the crate for another ten minutes or so. He may go to sleep. After all, little puppies sleep a lot more than they are awake.

If the puppy is sleeping, let him sleep until he wakes up. When he wakes up, go to him immediately and take him to his paper. Then, spend some time with the puppy.

Crate time is lengthened gradually. At about sixteen weeks of age, the puppy's maximum daytime stay is extended to about two hours. This depends on your puppy and his own schedule.

(2) Place the crate in a small room with an easily cleaned floor. A laundry room, bathroom, or kitchen would be ideal. The theory is to divide the puppy's small world into three parts. Place the crate in one corner of the room and spread newspaper in an opposite corner. As in paper training, leave a scented page on top. Place the puppy's water bowl and food dish in a third corner. Put the puppy in the crate, but leave the crate door open. At least the puppy will learn to appreciate the crate's security and will leave the crate to eliminate.

Accidents

Don't let an untrained puppy wander through the house unsupervised. Keep him next to you every minute of the day. If you're really busy, attach one end of a lead to the puppy and the other to your belt or your wrist. It's far better to have a week or two of restriction than a lifetime of corrections.

Even the best-mannered puppy, and older dogs, too, will have an occasional indoor accident. Your puppy will have elimination accidents until about six months old, but urinary tract infections can lead to accidental puddling at any age.

If the puppy does leave a puddle or a pile in the house, work harder at understanding why. Did you not get back in time? Is there a disruption in your puppy's life? Do you have a new baby or another dog? Go back to the basics. Watch the puppy more carefully. Rubbing the puppy's nose in his mess is disgusting, confusing, unfair, and ineffective. And hitting the puppy is out of the question.

Try harder to catch the puppy in the act of breaking the rules. The minute the objectionable behavior begins, get to the puppy as quickly as possible. Even while you're on the way, call out "No!" in a loud voice. Pick the puppy up, even though he's still dribbling, and carry him to the paper or outside, repeating, "No!" Once or at most twice should teach the lesson.

After the accident: If the puppy does wander onto your wall-to-wall carpet, an old fashioned solution for urine stains is kitchen cornstarch. First, blot the spot with paper towels. Use your foot for pressure. Change paper towels several times until you are sure the moisture is gone. Be sure the spot is completely dry, then layer on a generous amount of cornstarch. Leave the corn-starch on the spot overnight. Keep the puppy away from it. Once the cornstarch is dry, just vacuum it up.

A second remedy for rug spotting involves the use of diluted vinegar. Be very sure the rug is colorfast. If necessary, test a small corner before you begin. First, with a pad of paper towels, blot up all the urine you can. The spot must be as dry as possible. Then saturate the spot again with a mix of one part of vinegar with two parts of water. Try to add as much mixture as there was urine. Let sit five minutes then sponge up as much of the vinegar mixture as you can with an old towel. Cover with a pad of paper towels. Weigh down and let dry.

Once your puppy finds a spot in the house more to his liking, you may be sure he will head back in that direction the next time. Several companies manufacture a bacteria and enzyme combination stain and odor remover. When used immediately on carpets and upholstered furniture, this culture of friendly bacteria actually eats up and eliminates the organic matter. It also eliminates the problem of "repeats" by removing the odor. Never use a product with ammonia to cleanse a urine stain. It's the ammonia odor in the urine that lures the dog back to the spot.

Be a good neighbor: If you walk your puppy on a leash, remember to be fair to others. Curb your dog. Never let your puppy eliminate on the sidewalk. And once his duty is done, pick up after your puppy.

Exercising Your Puppy

Anyone who has experienced the enthusiasm of seven puppies set down in the backyard for the first time would be justified in wondering why puppies need special exercise times. The energy of that boundless and bounding brood soon spills over into a leaf chasing, tail tugging, no-holds-barred playtime.

One of the joys of puppy watching is sharing the enthusiasm of a healthy, friendly animal as he rushes headlong into new experiences. Exhausted and satisfied, the puppy will flop into the most comfortable, sun-dappled spot available and instantly fall asleep. In an hour or two, the cycle will repeat itself with as much enthusiasm as ever.

The time will come, however, at about four months, when the puppy's main concern is his aching gums, and a new cycle will set in. The puppy will sit for an hour chewing on stair treads, rocker rungs, the side of the house, bannister railings, and whatever comfortable target is around. Two new problems will have arisen. One, running exercise has slowed, and two, teething panic sets in as 42 sharp little teeth work their way to the surface.

Take your puppy for a long walk every day. Walk around the block—around several blocks. If you think it is better, put your puppy in a car and head for a park or open field. If you are a cyclist, your pup might like to run with you on a back roads excursion. In whatever manner you decide to exercise, work up to it gradually, and don't overdo.

Remember that, even at ten months, a Shar-Pei is still developing. His skeletal and musculature connections are still forming. The constant stress and pounding of running on a hard surface can take its toll on joints leading to complications later. Your puppy will want to keep up and will not realize it is hurting itself. It is up to you in this, as in so many other aspects of your pet's life, to do the thinking for both of you.

Puppy Games

Some games are exercises in themselves. These provide the puppy with contact and companionship with you while affording an outlet for that awesome puppy energy. The side benefits of discipline and procedure will help when you are both ready to move on to the next level of training.

You may start any of these games once you can get your dog's attention, and can put your dog in a "sit/stay" position. Success is most likely when your pet is at least six months of age.

Remember, your puppy has a short attention span and tires easily. Keep these games short and fun. Ten to 15 minutes at a time is plenty.

Find it: "Find it" can be so lively that it can keep the two of you playing longer than you planned. Because a successful search is always accompanied by a treat, your dog itself often will initiate the game.

Put your pet in a "sit/stay." (See The Basic Obedience Commands, page 71.) Say, "stay." Hold a treat at eye level. Say, "smell it!" Don't let your dog grab the treat. Now, place the treat on the ground beside you. Say, "find it!" Of course, Buddy will go straight for it. Let him have the treat and be very enthusiastic with your praise.

Your problem will be to keep Buddy in a "sit/stay" with the treat in plain sight. Be sure not to give in. If your pet breaks the stay, start over. The key is getting the dog to move on your command, "find it."

Now, select a toy, such as a dumbbell or a small ball. Again, put your puppy in a "sit/stay." Hold the object up and again say, "smell it." Move the object several feet away, in plain sight. Say "find it." Your puppy will go for it. Give a treat and a lot of praise.

Early socialization is key for all puppies.

The clue to success is to gradually escalate the difficulty of the find. When your puppy is ready, place the object on a higher level, a step, for instance, instead of the floor. Then, move the search to another room. First, leave it in plain sight. Then, conceal it behind a chair or sofa. Keep in mind that you are working at two levels here, the "sit/stay" and the search. Be sure to give your pet plenty of praise, and, in the beginning, always give a tasty treat. Later on, you will be able to move the search outdoors. You can dispense with the treat because the game will reformulate into the pleasure of the hunt.

Eventually, the puppy will respond to a word not associated with an object. "Buddy, where's the mouse? Find it!" results in a great deal of running about resulting in general commotion and enjoyment. And exercise.

Jump over: Although Shar-Pei are not noted for their high jump abilities, they are great bouncers. Your pet can be taught to enjoy a game of "jump over" and will become an enthusiastic player.

It should be easy to teach your pet to jump over a low hurdle to retrieve an object and to return that object to you. Again, start this game inside if you can. You will retain control and learning will be quicker.

Prop a 1-foot (30-cm) high board across a doorway, perhaps the doorway to your pet's sleeping quarters. Place a favorite chew toy on the other side of the barricade. Put your pet on a leash. Say "over" and pull gently on the leash. Use your most encouraging voice. If after several attempts, your pet still hesitates, jump over the board with him. When you both reach the other side, praise heartily and offer a food treat.

SHAR-PEI SOUNDBITES

The Shar-Pei does not need a large space in which to exercise but does need consistent daily activity such as walks on lead.

Every day, take a few minutes to reinforce the command. Place a treat or a toy on the other side of the board. Call your pet to you. Say "over." When the puppy jumps over, be ready with your praise.

Now move the game outside. Set a board up between two trees, for instance. Practice "over," remembering to give a lot of praise for a job well done. Although Shar-Pei can jump a 3-foot (0.9-m) barricade with little trouble, you don't want your puppy to strain. This is supposed to be a play and exercise game.

The game of "jump over" can be worked into "fetch," which is described below.

Fetch: Like the first two, this game is best started indoors. Although Shar-Pei are not known as retrievers, they enjoy retrieving games. Learning to bring an object to you is a game that most Shar-Pei handle with pride. One day, you will be able to send Buddy out for the morning paper with every expectation of getting it back in one piece, and only slightly damp.

First, start off with a favorite toy. An easy-to-carry dumbbell is great. Kneel at your puppy's side. Get its attention. Then, toss the object a couple of feet in front of both of you. Say "fetch!" Your puppy will run toward the toy.

The hard part will be getting the puppy to return the toy to you. That's why this game is best started indoors where you have an opportunity to correct mistakes right away. If Buddy runs off with the sock, or settles down to nibble on it, do whatever you can to get both the dog and the toy back. Call, whistle, encourage, coax. Don't chase the puppy. If necessary, walk in the other direction. Call the puppy again. When he comes, with or without the toy, praise lavishly. Go and get the toy yourself. If the puppy seems interested, try again.

"Fetch" works because, eventually, your puppy will learn that if you don't have the toy, he doesn't get to play anymore. Don't move this game outside until the puppy consistently returns the toy to you. At that point, you can change to a ball or a rolled newspaper.

Bad Habits and What to Do About Them

Behaviorists tell us that most problems are caused by boredom. A dog is by nature a social animal with definite needs. If these needs are frustrated, the dog will bark, dig, and engage in destructive behavior. Many of these pets wind up in animal shelters.

If you have a dog, it is up to you to spend time with him, train him, and love him until he is secure.

Aggressive Behavior

According to animal behaviorists, barking, biting, and fighting are natural signs of aggression. Although it is better to work with your dog when he is a puppy to prevent bad behavior habits from developing, troublesome behavior usually can be corrected.

Barking

Barking is normal behavior in dogs. Some puppies seem to be more vocally oriented than others. Some bark out of boredom. Others, instinctively ready to defend their territory, bark at some person, situation, or noise with which they are uncomfortable.

Frequently, dog owners encourage their pets to bark. They like to believe that their dog will alert them to unusual noises or people. Unless your dog is aggressive, your appearance at a window or on the porch will satisfy his anxiety about the distraction, and the barking will cease.

It is no secret that barkers left at home alone during the day annoy neighbors. Nighttime barkers are a sleep-inhibiting nuisance.

Correction of these problem barkers involves retraining the dog to ignore the stimulus. Both ultrasound devices and antibark shock collars can be effective. When the distraction of the ultrasound, for instance, closely follows the stimulus to bark, the dog's reflexes are reconditioned. It is encouraged to use silence as a response rather than barking.

Biting

Biters are a menace to unsuspecting postal workers, meter readers, uncautious children, and long-suffering veterinarians. Puppies that nip can develop into biters. Particularly if yours is an excitable puppy, avoid bouts of tug-of-war and heavy horseplay. Remember that attack dogs are trained by a trainer playing the role of agitator. Successively threatening movements by the agitator trigger the dog's defense reflexes. Observe your dog to see if he is receiving such stimuli.

Be consistent with the rules of the house with your puppy.

Destructive Chewing

Because chewing helps your pet to clean his teeth, promotes tooth development, and helps with jaw alignment, he should not be discouraged. Destructive chewing, a sign of boredom, is a problem. Providing your pet with special chew toys may help to redirect its energy.

If you catch your dog in the act of destructive chewing, say "No!" in a loud voice. If the dog stops or drops the object, take it away from the place and give the command, "sit," and a chew toy. After a few minutes, because he is being good, praise the puppy and tell him what a good dog he is.

Sprinkling bitter apple or hot pepper sauce on the chair rung, stair step, or table leg can help discourage these nibblers.

YOUR ADULT SHAR-PEI

The art of living with a healthy, adult Chinese Shar-Pei is comparable to sharing your home with an intelligent, robust, and inquisitive friend.

When you speak, your new friend will listen attentively. Her head will tilt, indicating interest. Her small ears will perk up. Her almond-shaped eyes, clear and free of irritation, will be bright and responsive. At mealtimes she will eat well and happily. When left alone, she will devise games and activities to keep herself amused until you return. She will keep one eye on the door and both ears alert for your footstep. She will be devoted to you and your family, neutral, and even standoffish with strangers, until properly introduced.

This friendly relationship is not an accident. It is special because both of you have worked to make it so. In the give and take of daily life, certain obligations are accepted on both sides. Primary among these responsibilities is teaching your pet the rules of the house.

Before you know it, you will be partners with a happy, well-adjusted adult Shar-Pei.

House Dog, Yard Dog

A Shar-Pei does not have to be a house dog, but still needs to be part of the family. The dog that lives primarily outdoors learns to enjoy the feel of grass and leaves under her feet. For that Shar-Pei's owners, housetraining is little more than reinforcing habits learned at her mother's side. A puppy is accustomed to eliminating away from its den. If trained to eat, sleep, and eliminate outside, she will be uncomfortable walking or resting on slippery inside flooring. An outdoor dog will stand at the door, whine, scratch, or otherwise let you know she needs to go outside. She will not want to come inside unless outdoor temperatures, wind, or noise levels cause her extreme discomfort, or unless she is lonesome. In that instance, early puppyhood training is a must for any pet. Our pets frequently come inside for companionship. If we ourselves go out, however, they will follow immediately.

A horse-coat Shar-Pei.

Exercising the Adult Shar-Pei

Some country pets are allowed to run free and receive boundless exercise chasing squirrels, falling leaves, and strange noises. For these, only the supervision of a stout fence is necessary.

Others, with less freedom to roam, must search out that open space in parks, on country roads, and playgrounds.

Increase the level of activity suggested for puppies to one suitable to the adult Shar-Pei. As noted earlier, watch your pet carefully. Don't overexercise.

The Indoor Pet

Although their ancestors were probably country dogs that lived in barns and yard kennels, it would seem that most of today's Shar-Pei are indoor pets. Pets confined to apartment buildings, or raised in yards without fencing, depend on daily walks to stay constitutionally fit. These confined animals, more than any other, require a carefully thought out exercise program performed on a routine basis.

If yours is a fenced-in yard, your indoor pet will get sufficient exercise if you let her play outdoors for several hours twice a day.

The Outdoor Pet

In situations such as a non-fenced yard, where you must keep your pets in an outdoor kennel, you should make specific arrangements for their comfort. Try to set up her outdoor kennel house in an out-of-the-way location, away from yard traffic. You will find that Princess will spend a great deal of time facing the back door or the side gate or wherever you first appear. Position the entrance of the kennel so the door will face that side if you can. If possible, set it against the side of the garage or against a solid structure to shelter it from winter winds and driving spring rains. Raise the floor of the kennel off the ground for extra comfort in summer. Some thoughtful owners put a window in their dog's house so she can see out.

Be sure the kennel is large enough so your pet can turn around, and small enough so that her own body heat can keep her comfortable in winter. A provision to add heat to the kennel on cold winter nights is a welcome touch. Even so, some nights you probably will have to give your pet further shelter, inside or in the garage, if yours is a harsh winter. A Shar-Pei's

Outdoor dogs should be well-protected from the elements.

short coat doesn't offer much protection against freezing temperatures.

Constructing an outside run: If you cannot fence your entire yard, why not consider a dog run enclosing the doghouse? A galvanized, 11-gauge, zinc-coated wire fence 8-feet (2.4-m) wide and 16-feet (5-m) long should give your Shar-Pei plenty of exercise room until you can take it out on a leash. Pet shops and catalogs carry ready-made runs that can be adapted to your backyard. Shade and a continuous water source are a must.

Grooming Your Shar-Pei

Although a Shar-Pei sheds very little, and is considered perfect "as is," she will appreciate your assistance in maintaining that perfection. Given daily care, your pet will not need frequent baths and will remain basically odor free. Daily, or at least every other day, brushing stimulates the skin, distributes oils, and removes dead hair. Use a moderate bristle brush, not a wire brush, and be sure to stroke with the lay of the coat.

That bristly coat seems to have a mind of its own. In lieu of shedding, both male and female Shar-Pei drop (blow) their coat twice a year, in spring and fall. Extra grooming attention will be needed at these times. In the female, the tension of first heat and the stress of whelping also can induce shedding.

If your Shar-Pei scratches or has bald spots, first have her checked by a professional for mange and allergies. If all checks out, consider her diet. Some Shar-Pei benefit by the addition

of one to two teaspoons of fatty acids such as omega-3 or omega-6 to her morning meal.

Bathing

Although Shar-Pei with skin problems benefit from frequent bathing, a healthy Shar-Pei needs a bath no more than once a month. When you do bathe your dog, use warm water and a gentle shampoo made for dogs.

Be considerate. A dog doesn't need or appreciate water in her ears or eyes. Before you begin, crumple a small wad of cotton and lightly plug each ear. Begin by creating a wet, soapy ring around the dog's neck. The soap will form a barrier to prevent fleas from crawling toward the dog's face and eyes. Shampoo the head and face next. Then work your way down the dog's back, legs, feet, and tail. Don't forget the toes. The

Children should be involved in caring for your Shar-Pei.

secret to a clean wash is a thorough rinse. Rinse and rinse some more.

Unless the day is exceptionally warm and sunny, dry your pet carefully and completely before letting it go outside. The Shar-Pei's short coat drys quickly. In the event of exceptionally cold weather, don't take chances with your pet's health. Shampoo your dog in the evening and keep her indoors. That way the dog's coat has overnight to dry.

Some Shar-Pei are troubled with dry skin. Consider adding an oil such as Alpha Keri or Skin So Soft to the final rinse. Afterwards, you might try a gentle rubdown with vitamin E or wheat germ oil. Some breeders have had success with lanolin cream.

You will want to be observant as to the skin reaction, if any, you get when you try any new product on your pet. Some Shar-Pei are extremely sensitive to product ingredients. Dogs have allergies just as people do.

Teeth and Nails

Feeding your pet dry kibble is a thoughtful way to keep her teeth cleaned. Bones make excellent toothbrushes. For her own health, see that your pet is provided with a Nylabone or other hard chewing bone once or twice a week.

Many owners brush their dog's teeth with a special brush and meat-flavored toothpaste. This removes lodged particles but does nothing for tartar. Tartar buildup is not normal. If you find tartar on your Shar-Pei's teeth, tell your veterinarian.

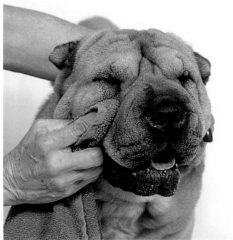

A clean pet is a happy pet.

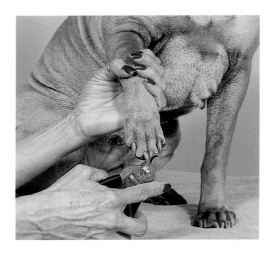

Trimming a Shar-Pei's nails.

If your Shar-Pei is a house dog, take a look at those toenail tips once a week or so, and keep them well trimmed. If you can hear a click when the dog walks on a wooden floor, it's time for a trim.

The Shar-Pei is not at ease unless she is in control. Attempting to clip the nails of an adult dog standing on three legs can develop into a battle of wills. For this reason, while your pet is still a puppy, be sure you spend a great deal of time grooming her, fussing over her, handling her ears, feet, and teeth, and trimming her nails. You can keep all the equipment you need to groom your Shar-Pei in a tack box. For more information, see page 56.

Ears

A dog's hearing is extremely acute. One study indicated that a sound you can't hear at 17 feet (5 m) can be heard by most dogs at 75 feet (23 m). It is extremely important to the animal's health that this remarkable hearing ability be retained.

One of the Shar-Pei's most beguiling features, the tiny ear flaps that lie tight against her head, can cause problems. On occasion, the ear canal itself is narrower than it should be. Because of poor air circulation caused by the dog's tight-fitting ear flaps, this interior canal is dark, warm, and moist. The stage is set for bacteria and yeast growth.

Check your pet's ears once a week. Clean the outer edges with a moistened cotton swab. Don't probe into the ear canal itself. Don't use

Shar-Pei dental health includes brushing teeth.

mineral oil to clean the ear flap, as it will collect and trap dirt. Commercial ear cleansers are available.

If you notice a discharge or smell a bad odor, see your veterinarian.

Eyes

The deep-set almond shaped eyes are another unique feature of the Shar-Pei. The standard calls for the eyes to be "sunken,"

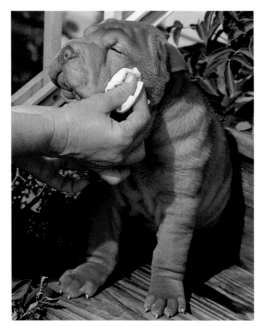

A Shar-Pei's wrinkles can hold dirt and food that may irritate the skin. Be sure to clean your Shar-Pei after meals.

which can lead to irritation, tearing, and eye rubbing.

You should pay special attention to your pet's eyes. If your Shar-Pei scratches or blinks or rubs one or both eyes frequently, or if the eyes water, consult your veterinarian. Entropion, a hereditary disease, is discussed in the Shar-pei Health Care chapter.

Mouth

The wrinkled Shar-Pei muzzle needs daily attention. Food can collect in the folds and creases of your pet's mouth. If this happens, you will notice a rancid odor as the food decays, and an increase in slobbering. You will

SHAR-PEI SOUNDBITES

The roundish interior shape of the mouth, responsible for the breed's firm bite, is commonly known as "Roof Tile Mouth."

have to stretch the mouth folds after each meal and clean and dry the area.

Identifying Your Shar-Pei

The lost and found columns are filled with advertisements offering rewards for a "children's pet," or an "older dog, needs medication, no collar," or a "family devastated, companion dog."

Until it happens to you, you seldom may consider the possibility of your pet straying or wandering. Even less does one consider thievery. And yet, when you read the classified section, you may realize that yours is only one of many show dogs and pet dogs reported missing every day.

The stories of Princess traveling 2,000 miles (3,000 km) to return to a family that moved cross-country are heartening. Most such real life tales, though, conclude on a dimmer note.

A brass plate engraved with your pet's name can assist, not deter, a thief. Buckle collars, of course, can be removed.

Many owners seeking more permanent identification choose to have their pets tattooed or to have a microchip implanted. The tattoo is etched on the inside of the dog's thigh, near its abdomen. The microchip, a tiny transponder about the size of a grain of rice, is gaining favor over tattoos. The chip, offered by HomeAgain, is placed under loose skin near the shoulder blade.

The cost varies depending on various factors, but is usually somewhere between $50 and $100 for chip and registry.

For a nominal fee ($12.50) the American Kennel Club registry provides lifetime recovery services for enrolled pets in their Companion Animal Recovery (CAR) program. In the past ten years, CAR has reunited 300,000 pets with their owners, reporting one reunion every seven minutes. Interested pet owners can find further information on these programs in the Resources section of this book.

Traveling with Your Shar-Pei

Travel is a part of modern life. You want your friend to be as welcome as you are. You need to teach her the basic rules of car travel early. As a puppy she can learn to ride in her crate and look forward to the adventure to be found in a new setting at the end of the day. Later, you both can be pleased to return home.

On occasion, however, you may be faced with a situation that requires special handling. Trips of longer duration, and overnight traveling in particular, call for ingenuity and advance preparation.

Car Travel

✔ Set up a travel kennel in the backseat. Add a chew toy. Put your dog in it.

✔ Don't leave right after a meal. Pack your dog's dish, a supply of food, and snacks. Carry a thermos of cold water with you.

✔ When you stop for a rest, give your Shar-Pei a break, too. Remember that the interior of a closed car, even one parked in the shade, can turn into an oven in a few minutes. Before

A crate keeps a dog safe when traveling.

leaving your dog, ask yourself if you would stay in the car under those conditions.

✔ Carry with you a list of hotels and motels that accept pets. An excellent Internet resource that includes suggestions, books, and articles for traveling with your pet can be found at the American Dog Trainers site *http://www.inch.com/~dogs/travel.html.*

Air Travel

Sometimes a job promotion involves a cross-country airplane ride. In the excitement of selling the house, shipping the furniture, and finding a new school for the children, don't forget to spend a few minutes reassuring

Reduce the stress of travel on your pet by planning ahead.

Princess. Air travel is no more a hardship on your Shar-Pei than it is on you or the children. In this instance, having a pet accustomed to a dog crate is a blessing.

Be sure your pet's shots are up-to-date. Carry your Shar-Pei's veterinarian records and health certificate on your person, not in your luggage.

Make your dog's reservation when you make yours. She will travel in the cargo space. Don't feed your dog within six to eight hours of a flight. Bring bowls, food, and water in your carry-on. Be ready to feed and exercise your pet at your destination.

Boarding Your Shar-Pei

Most veterinarians offer kennels at a reasonable cost. The staff, composed of conscientious animal lovers, will welcome your pet as a friend. You might use this time to have your Shar-Pei checked for parasites, have her nails clipped, or have her bathed. Be sure her immunizations, including bordetella are up to date.

You will want to bring some of the comforts of home: food, feeding dish, favorite toys, and supplements.

Registering Your Shar-Pei

Among the CSPCA's former responsibilities, now assumed by the AKC, is dog and litter registration. The AKC maintains an ancestral record of each dog, known as a stud book. Regulations for registration are specific. Upon your purchase of a registrable dog, you will receive a registration application provided by the litter's owner. The face of the application discloses the dog's breed, her sex, color, and date of birth, the names of her parents, her litter number, and the litter owner's name and address. On the reverse, the litter owner transfers ownership to you. Upon receipt of this application and the registration fee, the AKC will issue to you an AKC registration certificate.

Showing Your Shar-Pei

Many Shar-Pei owners are more than satisfied to have the quiet, solitary friendship of a loving, companionable dog. Together, the pair enjoy the peaceful camaraderie of quiet winter walks and boisterous autumn afternoons.

Some dogs and some owners, though, enjoy the show ring. When the lightweight show collar slips over the show dog's head, the ceremony begins. The duo trot easily and well through the show routines. If Princess has a stable personality, one neither shy nor aggressive, if her conformation is excellent, if she has never had eye tacking, both of you might enjoy showing off.

Attend several shows. Watch the dogs and their handlers. Then talk to one or two who impressed you with their love of the breed and make arrangements for further instruction.

What Does a Pedigree Mean?

Your dog's pedigree is her family tree. Compiled from CSPCA and AKC stud book records, a pedigree proves that for generations all of the dog's ancestors were of the same breed. In addition, a pedigree contains birth dates, coat colors, and any championships and obedience titles. Some of the abbreviations on your Shar-Pei's pedigree might be: CH (Champion), CD (Com-

panion Dog), and CDX (Companion Dog Excellent). For dog owners interested in breeding, a pedigree is essential. With this knowledge a breeder can predict with greater accuracy such critical variables as appearance, temperament, and conformation.

How to Read a Pedigree

The word pedigree derives from the French words for crane's foot, *pied de grue*. That is because some inspired searcher felt that the lines on a pedigree chart resembled bird tracks.

In each generation listed on the chart, the sire's (the father's) name appears first, above the dam's (the mother's) name.

The two-letter prefix followed by a six-digit number is the dog's registration number. The date next to this number is the month and year the dog's name was published in the stud book register.

Where to Obtain a Copy

Once you receive your Shar-Pei's registration certificate, you may request its pedigree from the American Kennel Club, 51 Madison Ave., New York, New York 10010. A three-generation pedigree will list 14 ancestors. A four-generation pedigree will list 30 ancestors. If you want to know the coat color of your Shar-Pei's ancestors, indicate this in your letter.

The Shar-Pei is shown in her natural state. Her bearing speaks for itself. Nevertheless, although the breed does not require a lot of clipping and grooming, assembling all the housekeeping gear in one place is an important first step. An equipment box, called a "tack" box by horse and dog folk, holds basic grooming necessities. Some handlers carry their gear in specially designed aluminum cases, others convert wheeled ice coolers, and still others search yard sales for old tackle and tool boxes.

Whatever your choice for the container, your content options are even more plentiful.

✔ **Soft bristle brush**—Daily brushing of that bristly coat allows you to watch for hot spots, allergic reactions and possible skin infections.

✔ **Narrow-tooth flea comb**—Summertime and hot temperatures are flea heaven. Particularly if yours is an outdoor pet, chances of her coming into contact with her nemesis the flea are greater.

✔ **Scissors**—Hair sprouts around the ears or between the toes can be problems. You can take care of them right away because your trimming scissors are right at hand.

✔ **Nail clippers**—Guillotine clippers do a good job on fast-growing nails.

✔ **Doggie toothbrush and toothpaste**—Some owners and their pets prefer finger toothbrushes over handled brushes. You may want to try pliable "edible" toothbrushes. Whichever you use, frequency and hamburger-flavored paste makes the job less stressful.

✔ **Treats**—Liver treats and natural cookies for "good boy" times are handy anytime.

✔ **Pet shampoo**—Any brand recommended by your veterinarian or the local fancy should be satisfactory.

✔ **Towels and hand cloths**—Wiping dribble, cleaning ears and forestalling shakedown showers are only some of the many uses for a stack of clean terry towels.

✔ **Bottled water**—For both of you.

✔ **Hand dryer**—Your dog will love it. Once it gets accustomed to the noise and the whoosh of the dryer you will find she loves to preen.

Tack Box Additional Tips

1. Daily brushing keeps the skin and coat in top condition. The procedure can be a time for you and your pet to bond. It is also a time to gently check for allergic reactions to items your pet encounters daily. Is it hay fever season for

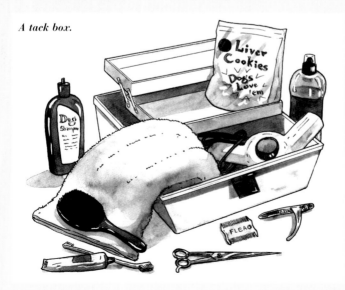

A tack box.

TACK BOX

you? Is the pollen count high? Your Shar-Pei might also have allergies. Be aware as you introduce new items into your pet's daily routine. Have you just had your carpet cleaned? Are you using a new doggie shampoo?

2. Dogs get cavities just like people do. Brush your dog's teeth at least twice a week. You will control plaque and tartar buildup and avoid future dental problems. The first week or two the puppy arrives to join your family is the best time to accustom both of you to the procedure. Don't use toothpaste made for people. Use a special toothpaste developed for dogs. Make the brushing a special bonding time. Keep up a running, comforting commentary while you brush. Be lively. Don't "take all day." Offer a special treat at the end of the session.

3. You might wish you had three hands when you blow-dry your dog: one to hold the dryer, one to brush and the other under your pet's chin. If you don't have a grooming table such as that used by professionals, try tucking the handle end of the dryer in the waistband of your jeans or under a belt. With a little practice this "third hand" works pretty well.

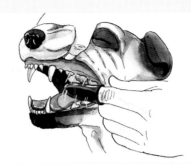

Brush your pet's teeth at least twice a week.

Remember to set your dryer's heat level on "low" or "warm." A setting you can tolerate will burn a dog.

4. If your dog absolutely hates having her ears cleaned or her hair sprouts plucked, try to do the job in stages. Using a cotton ball, sprinkle a little talc on the hairs. It makes them easier to grab. And remember, don't pluck too many at one sitting.

5. "Practice makes perfect" is as true for grooming as for showing. You and your pet will be better off because you both learned. *"I hear and I forget, I see and I remember, I do and I understand."* Chinese proverb.

NUTRITION

Shar-Pei are not finicky eaters. They have been known to eat ice cream, the ice cream cone, and the napkin wrapping; to consume a tray of hamburgers, the buns and, well, you get the idea.

For your dog's continuing good health, from puppyhood through old age, you should feed Buddy properly on a regularly established meal-time schedule. Proper feeding doesn't necessarily mean that you must become an instant nutritionist, only that you have a basic knowledge of your pet's nutritional needs. Proper nutrition doesn't mean depriving your pet of treats and snacks. It does mean keeping in mind the value (or deficit) of such snacks and using them as part of your overall feeding program. Most of all, proper feeding means training your pet to eat what you set before it.

Most of those that had to be coaxed into eating were babied, petted, and eventually spoiled into their bad eating habits by indulgent owners who plied them with tidbits and human-type snacks. (If you already have allowed your pet to develop a taste for an unbalanced diet, and you want to get its nutri-

The foundation of a healthy, happy Shar-Pei is its nutrition.

tion back on a healthy track, see Changing Your Pet's Diet on page 65.)

If yours is a young Shar-Pei, just beginning life's journey, you will want him to develop good eating habits. In order to achieve a happy medium, you need to provide your pet with the right amount of the right kinds of food at the proper times.

Recognizing a Healthy Diet

Your pet should have, on a daily basis, fresh water, proteins, carbohydrates, fats, vitamins, and minerals, just as you should.

Keep a fresh water supply available at all times. He will know when it has to replenish the water in his system and he will know when he has had enough.

Proteins, Fats, and Carbohydrates

A daily diet containing top quality proteins is important to your pet's good growth and development. In addition to serving as the body's basic building tools, proteins play a key role in the canine immune system, a most important consideration for this breed. Therefore, it is essential that 20 to 25 percent of the adult Shar-Pei diet consist of protein foods. The percentage variance comes with your dog's age and current health status. Inadequate protein levels can result in weight loss, a dull coat, hair loss, and, eventually, death.

Fifty percent of your Shar-Pei's daily diet should be composed of carbohydrates. Remember, a dog that does not receive enough carbohydrates in his diet automatically will convert proteins to carbohydrates. This self-manufacturing can then cause a protein deficiency that will only add to your pet's problems. A carbohydrate deficit, by the way, is rare in dogs that eat any commercially prepared dog food.

Because fat contributes twice as much energy as either protein or carbohydrates, many nutritionists suggest that fats and fatty foods make up the last 20 percent of your pet's daily diet.

Special Feeding Requirements

Your puppy's nutritional needs are very different from what his requirements will be six years down the road. At different times of his life along that road, his dietary needs will vary. If yours is a female, she will require a special diet when pregnant or nursing a litter. A six-year-old Shar-Pei, approaching middle age, might be ill or overweight. Your veterinarian can guide you through these changes.

Feeding a Puppy

Puppies grow rapidly and their diet should change also. First consider the seven- to eight-week-old puppy just entering a new home.

Remember that you are going to feed your puppy a daily diet containing about 30 percent protein, 20 percent fat, and the rest, carbohydrates. Your choices will include a homemade diet, and at least three different types of commercial foods.

Set up a regular feeding schedule. A puppy this age will want to eat three, sometimes four, times a day. His digestive system is not ready to consume the large amounts required for twice a day feeding. His stomach is too small to hold much, anyway, and as he is growing so rapidly he always seems hungry. A typical mealtime schedule is 7 A.M., noon, 5 P.M., and 10 P.M.

Healthy puppies are good eaters.

Set up a regular feeding schedule.

Shar-Pei do not mature until they are at least fifteen months old. The high protein levels of the puppy formulas are important considerations that must not be forgotten. If your puppy is thriving, he should be fed the same diet at least throughout his first year of life, just more of it. Usually, the feeding directions on the package can be followed, but a sensible rule of thumb is: Feed a puppy up to his appetite. In other words, divide the amount the puppy will consume each day into three or four equal amounts and serve that amount at each meal.

By the time your pet is six months of age, the number of meals per day can be reduced to two. This twice a day feeding can be continued for the lifetime of the dog as long as he is doing well and other considerations (health and weight, for instance) do not enter in.

Feeding Older Shar-Pei

Most veterinarians say that the Shar-Pei is a canine senior citizen by the time he is eight years old. Nevertheless, your pet, with proper care, can live and enjoy life well into the double-digit age range. It is up to you to prepare your old friend, through proper feeding habits, to enter old age with the dignity and well-being he deserves.

Lowering your dog's fat intake and watching his overall calorie count can also help immeasurably in increasing its life span.

If you feed a dry food, and your pet seems to be having trouble eating it, try soaking the kibbles in warm water until soft. Check his teeth for tartar or disease. Older dogs may have dental problems associated with tartar

buildup resulting in bone and tissue deterioration. A visit to the veterinarian will be in order.

Feeding the Overweight Dog

Some authorities say that over 50 percent of the general dog population are obese. Obesity, with all its associated problems, detracts from your pet's appearance. Instead of the handsome, self-confident Shar-Pei of legend, the overweight dog is physically slow and awkward. He is easily fatigued.

Low calorie, professionally prepared dog foods are a boon to both the overweight dog and its owners. These balanced preparations contain a minimal amount of fat and very adequate amounts of proteins and carbohydrates.

Note the famous hippo mouth.

Do count carefully the added calories of the doggy biscuits and treats you provide. These typically bone-shaped baked starch products contain from 18 to 20 calories each.

The Ailing Shar-Pei

Those illnesses and diseases to which the Shar-Pei is most prone are discussed in the Shar-Pei Health Care chapter. Some of these, including malabsorption, amyloidosis, bloat, and some skin and allergy problems, respond to dietary treatment. Your veterinarian will assist you.

Types of Food

Dog food manufacturers usually produce the same basic formulas in three different forms: (1) dry (dehydrated, kibbled), (2) semimoist (chunked, preformed), and (3) canned. Nutritional values within the same brand are often equal. The basic variances are consistency, odor, and percent of water.

Homemade

Because of the wide availability of high-quality dried dog kibble, fewer and fewer owners go to the expense and effort of preparing dog food at home. Yet owners of allergy-prone pets and pets with unusual dietary needs have been successful at duplicating a commercial diet.

As owners become more adept at managing their own nutrition, the BARF diet for dogs has gained in popularity. BARF (Biologically Appropriate Raw Food) enthusiasts feed their pets raw chicken wings, ground lamb, whole fish, boiled eggs (shell on), table scraps, and a variety of vegetables. Sweet potatoes, broccoli, snap beans, carrots, and seedless apples round out the week's diet. As with any dietary change, watch your pet carefully. If your Shar-Pei shows signs of gas, diarrhea, or vomiting, remove the offending food from his diet immediately.

Several nutrition books and Internet sites offer complete directions and analyses for homemade mixes. If you decide to take your pet's nutritional needs into your own hands, you would be wise to consult one of these, particularly one recommended by your veterinarian or your breed club.

Commercial

Promotional literature adorns the walls of veterinary offices, feed stores, pet shops, and grocery outlets. Pricing varies with the type of food, the quantity purchased, endorsements, protein levels, and advertising costs, for instance. What should you do now?

How to select a commercial dog food:
First, read the labels. The Association of American Feed Control Officials requires that a guaranteed analysis and a list of ingredients label be placed on the outside of all dog food packages. You are looking for the right proportion of protein, carbohydrates, fats, vitamins, and

SHAR-PEI SOUNDBITES

Dogs have well-developed taste buds easily perceiving sweet, salty, and sour.

minerals for your pet at its current stage of development.

If the label states that the food is complete, or balanced, this means that it contains all the nutrients required by a dog, and in the proper balance. The first label states the minimum and maximum levels of protein, fat, fiber, moisture, and other ingredients. The second label lists the ingredients in descending order of quantity. Don't forget to look at the moisture content, usually the last item on the first label. You are checking to see how much you will be paying for water. Then, write down and study your results.

The reality is that your own dog will be the best test of a product. If you choose to feed one of the "plain wrapper" (generic) dog foods, watch your dog carefully and be prepared to provide food and vitamin supplements as needed.

In addition, observe your dog's stool output for a few weeks. Poor quality protein and too much indigestible fiber result in watery, mushy, foamy stools. In better quality dog foods, more of the food is absorbed by the dog, thus producing fewer, firmer stools.

Canned: Canned dog foods are blended and cooked and sterilized in a sealed can. About 50 percent of the protein comes from meat or poultry products. The remaining protein can be from eggs, fish, or dried milk. Dried skim milk and dried buttermilk, for example, are favorite

What Not to Feed Your Pet

Food to Avoid	Reason
Anything fried	too much fat
Anything chocolate	may cause racing heart, hyperactivity
Whole corn kernels	indigestible
Onions and garlic	may cause anemia
Raw eggs	may cause skin and hair problems, salmonella
Cakes, pies, desserts	may cause obesity, dental problems
Fish, poultry, or pork bones	may cause obstruction or laceration of digestive system

additives. The carbohydrates in canned food usually are derived from corn, barley, or wheat. One can of food usually contains about 450 calories.

Semimoist: The softer dog foods known as semimoist consist of approximately 25 percent water. They need no refrigeration even when opened. These products are relatively odorless and are convenient to handle. A 6-ounce (170-g) pouch or patty contains the equivalent calorie count to a 1-pound (454-g) can of dog food.

Dry: Dry dog foods are usually granules, pellets, or flakes that have been homogenized and cooked. Each pellet contains a mix of meat meals, grain, and vegetable products. Vitamin and mineral supplements are added.

Dog biscuits, hide bones: Most dogs love baked dog biscuits. Used as snacks and as training treats, these starchy products can be a diversion for your pet. Just be sure to include the calorie count (which can be as high as 20 calories apiece) to your pet's daily diet.

Some veterinarians caution owners not to give rawhide to older dogs. Many pets tear off and swallow large chunks of rawhide, which on occasion has settled in the intestine causing a potentially dangerous blockage.

How Often? How Much?

Weaned puppies from three to six months of age should be fed morning, noon, and evening. Be consistent with mealtimes. When the puppy is about six months old, you can make a decision about a permanent feeding schedule. Your pet can adjust to your schedule and will thrive on twice a day, once a day, or self-feeding mealtimes.

Self-feeding

Large, vermin-proof bins can be conveniently filled with a quantity of dry dog food, which is dispensed as the dog feeds. Many owners use these self-feeders with confidence. Although a mature Shar-Pei usually will not overeat when self-feeding, keep an eye on your pet's waistline.

Self-watering dishes are on the market, too. These devices connect to an ordinary outdoor faucet. A control valve regulates the amount of water in the dish. As the dog drinks, the valve opens and raises the water level when necessary. Be sure the water reservoir is in the shade.

Changing Your Pet's Diet

If your Shar-Pei is accustomed to eating doughnuts for breakfast, or pepperoni pizza for

A Shar-Pei puppy should eat about three times a day. You can cut his meals down to two as he enters adulthood.

supper, you might want to change his eating habits. Likewise, if you are planning a vacation, you might want to feed another type of food for traveling convenience. Perhaps you simply want to make the change to a different brand of food altogether. In any case, be sure to make changes gradually. Accustom your pet to the new diet over at least a week's period. The first two days, feed one part new food and three parts old diet. The third through fifth day, mix approximately half and half. The last days, offer three parts new diet and one part old food.

Keep an eye on your pet's stools, his actions, and activity level. If he accepts the new food, and if his digestive system seems stable, continue with the new diet.

What should you do if your pet refuses to eat what you set before it? Suppose he sniffs the bowl of kibble and walks away. If your pet refuses the new food, don't worry. If you are convinced that this dietary change is in your pet's best interests, you can wait it out. Take the food away if you like, throw it away if necessary, and try again at the next meal. Be sure always to keep plenty of fresh water available.

A healthy dog won't starve himself. Once you have convinced your dog, and the point is important, that this new flavor is what mealtime will consist of from now on, he will consume every bite with evident relish.

Finicky Eaters

Shar-Pei are not ordinarily fussy eaters. If, from the beginning, you feed your pet a high-quality kibble, with occasional added treats, he will eat heartily all his life.

Finicky eaters result by presuming a dog should eat what you eat. A lot of what you may eat isn't even good for your pet. You shouldn't give your dog fried potatoes, pie, or chocolate candy, for instance. It is better to train your pet to eat what you set before it. A puppy reared on a diet of dry kibble will enjoy every bite.

People think the dog may get tired of that same old diet. He does not. A dog can taste all the flavors in a kibble. Just try to add a little pill to a bowl of dry dog food and see what's left rolling around when the dog has finished.

OBEDIENCE TRAINING

A dog is an intelligent animal. Although limited in her ability to reason, she can think, and based on that thinking ability, can make decisions. Within the limits of her understanding a smart dog makes every effort to obey.

A dog is likewise an instinctively loyal animal, one eager to please. She is also a social animal, feeling most comfortable when in the presence of the one she respects, actively identifying with and seeking the approval of its chosen leader.

A thinking dog soon learns that this balm of approval with all its consequent benefits is withheld in response to her own actions. Obedience training helps dogs achieve these important objectives. The function of obedience training is to teach a willing dog how to behave in public and in private. Obedience training can prevent car chasing, cat killing, night barking, fear biting, and the myriad of undisciplined annoyances that turn household pets into neighborhood terrors.

Teaching these commands is not an easy matter. Learning the proper responses requires patience and persistence from both of you.

Nobody likes a disobedient dog. Obedience training begins early.

Once you live with an obedience-trained dog, however, and once you see how delightful life can be when you say "no"—and "no" it is—you will appreciate the effort.

Before You Begin

Princess' outlook on life, her confidence, and your relationship is shaped by the disciplined way in which you handle her training. Because each Shar-Pei is different in temperament, intelligence, and ability, successful trainers first evaluate a dog's natural inclinations and then adapt their methods to these aptitudes. Some of the guidelines include:

✔ Be observant. Most Shar-Pei are loyal, loving, and eager to please. Acquire a clear insight into your own pet's temperament and abilities.

✔ Don't use harsh training methods. Gentle, positive persuasion works best. Correct your dog as you would a child, with love. A disgusted voice can be discipline enough.

TIP

Liver Treats
½ pound (1.1 kg) beef liver
2 tsp. (10 g) garlic powder
1 tsp. (5 g) salt
2 cups (235 ml) water

Add salt and garlic powder to the water. Bring to a rolling boil. Add the liver. Reduce heat and simmer about 25 minutes or until liver is fork tender. Remove from water and let cool. Dice into ½ inch (1 cm) cubes. Refrigerate. Will keep for two weeks.

✔ Give both rewards and corrections immediately. Your puppy grew up expecting immediate corrections. The puppy's mother nuzzled and licked her when she was good, and growled and snapped when teaching a lesson.
✔ Don't be impatient, don't expect miracles.
✔ And do persevere. Once you start a lesson, keep repeating it until the dog understands.

Food Training: Yes or No?

Some trainers use food as an incentive for obedience, especially when training puppies. Other trainers insist that love and discipline are all that are necessary. When hugs and pats, especially in the early training stages, are reinforced by an accompanying food treat, food becomes a positive motivation. A dog learns to interact between an activity on its part and the reward received.

Most dogs adore training food. These treats, such as dog biscuits or boiled liver, are a high-light of their day. Food training focuses the dog's attention on a real, tangible reward. If you hold up a piece of food, or reach for the treat jar, a smart dog will sit in front of you and try to anticipate what it is you want her to do to attain the treat.

Training Treats

Many owners reserve doggy biscuits, pieces of last night's T-bone, or chips of hard cheese as reward food. Each of these has its place. Use what comes to hand. But the time will come when you might like to make your own training treats.

If you are a lifelong liver hater, you may be interested to know that one of your dog's favorite treats is going to be liver. At every pet show one vendor usually does a booming business selling bags of homemade liver squares. Take a hint from these professional trainers. Try training with garlic-flavored liver (see Tip box).

Training Schedules

Although both you and your new friend can learn much in the first six months of life together, serious obedience training should wait until your Shar-Pei is at least six or seven months old. Before that time the dog will be handicapped by her youth. When you do begin training, however, keep the following guidelines in mind:
✔ Dogs are creatures of habit. Set up a schedule and follow it. Work at the same times every day.
✔ Hold sessions twice a day, for not longer than 15 to 20 minutes each time.
✔ The puppy should have just one master. Let one person be the trainer and let other family members be the support team.

✔ Don't work if you're in a bad mood. Follow each session with at least ten minutes of fun.

Once You Begin

By the age of six months, your puppy is accustomed to the feel of a light leather or webbed nylon buckle collar. When you and Princess are ready to begin obedience training, however, you will want to purchase a light-weight metal training collar and either a metal or a webbed leash.

This training collar, commonly called a choke collar, is one of your most valuable training tools. The collar's common name, "choke," is misleading. The purpose of the collar is to get your dog's attention. When collared and cor-rected properly, the dog will not and should not choke. One end of the collar traditionally remains attached to the leash and is removed with the leash when the training session is fin-ished. Free running pets have been injured when loose choke collars catch and hang on obstacles in the field.

The trick to putting on a choke collar and leash is not difficult to master if you remember to face the dog when collaring her. Place the leash with the choke collar attached in your right hand. With the index finger of your left hand pick up the free hanging ring. Using your right hand, drop a section of the choke collar (with the leash still attached) through the free ring. Face the dog. When you hold the collar and leash up to the dog's head the shape will resemble the capital letter "P." with the leash forming the stem of the "P." (When you pull the choke collar over the dog's head the ring that is attached to the leash lies counterclockwise over the dog's neck. The leash falls free down the

Alert and ready.

right side of the dog's head.) Now, adjust the collar so that it sits high on the dog's neck, just behind the ears. Check the position by pulling the leash taut. A good, swift correction will tighten the collar immediately. When you release the pressure, the collar will hang free. If it doesn't, remove the collar, review the proce-dure, and try again.

If your puppy persists in leading you instead of letting you set the pace, a soft nylon head collar may be just the thing to put you back in the lead. It's not a muzzle, but a head control that puts pressure to the back of the dog's neck that prevents pulling, lunging, and choking.

Your Training Voice

The right tone of voice, the proper words at the appropriate time, and easy-to-read body language are your most important training tools.

Your training voice is your ally. Your dog can't understand many of your words. She easily learns to pay attention to your tone of voice. Listen to yourself as you train. Listen to a trainer you admire. Many successful trainers project two completely different tones of voice to their dogs.

If a trainer's everyday voice is naturally high pitched, that trainer works hard to develop a low, commanding tone when correcting. When praising, trainers usually adapt a happy, loving, singsong voice quite unlike their regular speaking tones.

You, too, can cultivate a stern, no-nonsense voice when you give a correction. Put some authority into your voice. You may have to correct your pet often for the same problem. A Shar-Pei can be stubborn. Be stubborn yourself. Don't give up your position as leader. Don't get angry, just be firm.

Then, cultivate a different tone for praise. That voice of praise can make a puppy feel like she is the sweetest, brightest, best behaved dog ever born. In an attempt to hear that praise again, a puppy will follow the trainer anywhere and perform any task she is assigned.

Once your training voices are in place, don't forget to talk to the dog with your body, too. Many verbal commands can be accompanied by hand and/or whistle signals. Your goal is to teach your dog to watch you as well as to listen to you. Many trainers soon drop the verbal command altogether.

Remember body language when correcting, too. When you give a correction to your dog, don't relax your body. Be stiff and remote. If the correction warrants it, stand up, then turn away, and avert your eyes for a while. To the contrary, when you praise your pet, use happy body language. Some trainers jump up and down after a breakthrough. Others clap and applaud. Some trainers of smaller breeds end a successful session by accepting a hug right back when their pet jumps into their outstretched arms. You can throw your arms around your dog, snuggle and pat and praise her. Always end a training session with a few minutes of play and fun.

Clicker Training

Click, treat! Click, treat! Click, treat! What is this clicker thing all about? The clicker is a small metal strip that emits a unique sound when bent. The sound gets the dog's attention and a quick treat keeps that attention active. Its advocates call it "operant conditioning" and tout it as the best training device to come along in years. Loosely, the term "operant conditioning" means setting a behavior pattern using action and consequence. Basically, you, the trainer, want a specific action from your pet. When you get that action you quickly reward her.

Clickers can be purchased at pet stores and usually come with a set of instructions. Books and videos can be invaluable sources of ideas and encouragement, but the best training tool is active participation in a local beginner's class. After all, you and your Shar-Pei deserve the best.

Three more reminders before you begin:
✔ Insist on obedience. Try not to let the dog get away with not obeying you.
✔ Use as few words as possible: one and two word commands are best. In addition to the "command" words for the five basic obedience situations, "sit," "come," "heel," "stay," and

Down!

"down," your pet can understand and will learn to respond to: "watch," "okay," "enough," "no more," "off," "give," "drop it," "good," "move," "take it," "don't jump," "jump in," "kennel up," "let's go," and "wait."

✔ Remember to praise or correct immediately after the action. If your dog performed well, praise her thoroughly and immediately. If your dog required corrections, correct immediately, and when the problem is over, follow that correction with praise.

The Basic Obedience Commands

Each of the following commands is begun on a leash. Because it is so important not to let your dog disobey a command, don't try these commands off a leash until you are very confident you can make your dog obey them. When you do go off the leash and the dog even looks like she isn't going to obey you, step in right away. Correct the dog before she has a chance to disobey. Give the command again. Be sure she obeys by returning to leash training if necessary.

As a matter of form, precede the moving commands ("come" and "heel") with your dog's name ("Princess, come.") When you give a stationary command ("sit," "stay," and "down"), omit your dog's name. This habit works in your favor because when your dog hears her name she knows you want her to prepare to move.

Your dog should obey a command until released. To release, tell your puppy "okay" and give her a quick pat. Remember the pointer about keeping your commands uniform. When you release your dog from a "stay," for instance, don't say "okay" one time, and "good" later. Once your dog is released, give her a pat, a treat, and a rousing round of praise. Spend a few minutes playing with your pet. Put on your most friendly voice and tell her what a good puppy she is.

Sit!

"Sit," known as the attention-getting command, is one of the easiest commands for your Shar-Pei to learn. Because "sit" is so useful, and so easy to teach, many trainers use it as the basis of any training.

Put your Shar-Pei on your left side, on a leash. Hold the leash in your right hand. Command "sit." (Do not use your dog's name.) Pull up on the leash and press down gently on the dog's hindquarters with your left hand. The dog will sit. Praise it.

Within a day or two, you won't have to press her down on the dog's hindquarters. Then your left hand will be free to give the hand signal with the verbal command. Hold your left hand stiffly in front of your dog's face, index finger pointed at the dog. Say "sit."

Many dog owners are not interested or think they do not have the time to teach their dogs the full range of obedience commands. Most of these indicate they would be very happy if their dog would just obey the command to "come." This is understandable, but because "come" is the easiest command for your dog to disobey once she is out of your physical range, "come" must be taught within the disciplined framework of obedience training. The basis for that frame is "sit."

Sit
✔ Verbal Command: "Sit"
✔ Hand Signal: Left hand up, index finger pointed toward the dog
✔ Whistle Signal: One short beep
✔ Pointers:

Come
✔ Verbal Command: "Princess, come."
✔ Hand Signal: Arms outstretched
✔ Whistle Signal: The whistle signal should be a beep-beep-beep, not a single prolonged blast. Start whistling immediately after you shout the command and continue the whole time the dog is coming to you.
✔ Pointers:

Because "come" is a command that must be obeyed, begin the training with your dog on a leash. Don't try "come" off the leash unless you are very sure the dog will obey you. If you let your puppy know that she can disobey, you are setting yourself up for problems later on.

Make the invitation to "come" attractive. Play with your Shar-Pei she comes. Give her a treat and a hug.

Don't ever ignore a dog that has obeyed the "come" command. Praise and play with the dog, no matter how long she took to come in.

Stay!

Never correct or discipline your dog after she finally returns. The dog will not understand the correction. If your dog did not return promptly when called, refresh her memory with leash training.

You must be sure that you retain the position of teacher (leader) and your dog the position of student.

Heel

✔ Verbal Command: "Princess, heel."
✔ Pointers:

Place the puppy in a "sit" at your left leg. Step off on your left foot (the foot closest to your puppy). Pat your leg. Give a light tug on the leash if necessary. As you walk, keep up a stream of talk and praise. Use your special praise voice. "What a good dog! That's a good puppy! Princess is a good dog! Look at us go. Let's go, Princess. Here we go! Good girl!"

✔ Give your dog no option. Keep a short leash. Walk in a straight line. Your dog will fol-low. Later, you can change course, stop, reverse. When you do, lean slightly in the direction of the turn. Pat your leg again.

✔ Don't drag the dog. Don't let the dog drag you. When you have to make a correction, do so with a slight tug on the leash and immedi-ately release the chain. Then praise your pet for obeying. The mildly uncomfortable correction gets the dog's attention. The praise is music to her ears.

Practice heeling on a leash until the two of you can move in circles, around corners, and among other dogs without having to give or receive a correction. Don't move to off-leash heeling until you are confident.

Stay

✔ Verbal Command: "Stay."
✔ Hand Signal: Left arm out, palm up in the "traffic control" stance
✔ Pointers:

Put your dog on a leash in a sit position at your left foot, facing forward. Gather the leash in your right hand. Command "stay." Put your left hand in front of the puppy's nose (even touching the muzzle at first).

Step away from the dog beginning first with your right foot. (Which foot you use is very important because you already have trained your puppy to identify a *left* foot start with the "heel" command.) Now, take one, or at most two, steps away. Keep your hands on your dog, if necessary to keep her from following.

Watch carefully and be ready to correct immediately at the first hint of movement.

Always end a training session with a few minutes of play and fun.

Keep the stay short—under 30 seconds at first. Say "okay" to release, and give your dog a lot of praise.

When you are sure your dog won't break on a short stay, try a longer stay. Try a longer

leash. Be ready to jump back. Your dog will want to follow you. Don't let her move.

Test your dog's "stay." Stand at the end of a 6-foot (1.8-m) leash. Say "stay" and tug on the leash. Really pull hard. Your dog should tug back. She should not move. Release. Say "okay," and praise.

When your dog holds this stay, try a "stay" off the leash. Be ready to go back on the leash at the first sign of disobedience.

Down

✔ Verbal Command: "Down."
✔ Hand Signal: Left arm outstretched, arm and palm move down as command is given
✔ Pointers:

Put your Shar-Pei on a leash. Give the "sit" command. Then, very deliberately and slowly, say "down."

"Down" is difficult for the puppy to understand. The posture signals submission, all the more reason to be firmly in control. Give the command. Then, using your left hand, apply pressure to your dog's shoulders. Say "down" again.

Keep your pet down for 30 seconds. Release your pressure. Say "okay," praise and treat. Good job!

Training Problems

Be sure your puppy understands what you want. Be sure she relates the punishment to the misbehavior.

Correct sloppy, unreliable responses immediately. If you have to repeat a command, if Princess takes her good old time coming to you, or worse, doesn't come at all, it's time for some extra work.

At the first signs of disobedience, particularly off the leash, go back at least one step. Be firm. Look your dog in the eye.

Unrealistic Expectations

Seasoned trainers don't expect perfection from a puppy until she is at least one year old. This doesn't mean that a well-trained puppy can't earn a Companion Dog degree at seven months. Many have. It just means that the average owner-handled family Shar-Pei often has other things to think about.

Rally

The new AKC Rally workout is an entry-level exercise designed for dogs and their owners working as a team. Much to the amusement and amazement of spectators, the teams rapidly traverse a deftly designed series of hurdles, turns, about-faces and jumps showcasing the dog's ability to follow hand or verbal instructions. Devotees place Rally somewhere between Good Citizen and true Obedience trials. The audience rates Rally as some of the best fun ever for handler and dog.

AKC Obedience Trial Regulations

The function of Obedience competition is to demonstrate the usefulness of the purebred dog as a companion, not just her ability to follow specified routines.

AKC Obedience Trials are divided into three levels of competence: novice, open, and utility. Proficiency at each level must be certified by three different judges. For further information, contact the American Kennel Club, 51 Madison Avenue, New York, New York, 10010.

You and your dog are a team. When both of you understand the rules of the game, life is pleasant, you can have a ton of fun and will be welcome members of the community.

In 1989, the AKC instituted a Canine Good Citizen program that recognizes well-trained pets. You and your pet earn this award by working together to learn ten basic obedience-friendly actions. As an owner you will be asked to sign a *Responsible Dog Owners Pledge* agreeing to take care of your pet's health, safety, exercise, and training.

Many breed clubs offer training lessons. Check listings in your community. You surely will find responsible dog owners willing to help you learn the program.

The Basics

The Good Citizen test is in ten parts. Your dog is on-leash at all times. You may talk to her, encourage her, hand out treats and otherwise be sure she is comfortable with the proceedings. When both of you are ready, proceed to the first station.

• **Station 1: Accepting a friendly stranger**—The evaluator will walk up to you and, ignoring your dog, offer a friendly greeting. Your pet must not show any discomfort,

and must not break position and try to go to the evaluator.

• **Station 2: Sitting politely for petting**—The evaluator pets your dog on the head and body. Again, the dog must not show any resentment or shyness.

• **Station 3: Appearance**—The evaluator inspects the dog to see if she is clean and well-groomed. The dog must appear to be healthy, with proper weight and appearance. The evaluator softly brushes the dog's coat, lightly examines the ears and gently picks up each front foot.

• **Station 4: Out for a walk**—Now you will leave the station for a brief walk on-lead. The evaluator will call out a right turn, a left turn, and an about turn with at least one stop in between.

• **Station 5: Walking through a crowd**—During this walk, your dog must pass close to several people. She is allowed to show some interest in the others but must continue to walk with you and must not strain on-leash.

• **Station 6: "Sit" and "Down" on command and staying in place**—This station will provide a 20-foot leash. You will put your dog in a "Sit" or "Down," and command her to "Stay." You will then turn and walk the length of the leash.

Walking through a crowd.

GOOD CITIZEN AWARD

Accepting a friendly stranger.

Reaction to another dog.

• **Station 7: Coming when called**—At this point, while 20 feet from your dog, turn to face your pet and call her to "Come."

• **Station 8: Reaction to another dog**—At this station, you will meet either the evaluator or another handler. The two of you will stop, shake hands, and continue on for about 10 feet. Neither dog should go to the other dog or her handler.

• **Station 9: Reaction to distraction**—The evaluator will present two distractions such as dropping a chair, a crutch or cane, rolling a crate dolly past the dog, or having a jogger run in front of the dog. The dog should not panic, try to run away, show aggression, or bark.

• **Station 10: Supervised separation**—The evaluator will say something like, "Would you like me to watch your dog?" and take hold of your dog's leash. You will go out of sight for three minutes. Your dog should not bark, whine, pace, or be extremely agitated or nervous.

When your pet receives this Award, you should both be proud. It is not given lightly. It is one more sign of the bond of friendship between you.

Reaction to distraction.

*You are your dog's best friend.
Your dog's second best friend
is the combination of your
veterinarian and timely
vaccinations.*

The information in this chapter is not intended to be used as a substitute for calling your veterinarian, but as support for your own good judgment on when to call.

If you are like most dog owners, you put a palm to the puppy's nose as a first health check. This is not always a reliable guideline. Although a dog's nose usually is cold and wet, a dry nose itself is not necessarily a sign of illness. Watch for other signs. Sometimes a personality or an appetite variance will be the first indication. Obvious signs, such as hair loss or intestinal problems, will alert you even earlier.

The bottom line is, as always, be observant. Know your Buddy. If he has a dry nose, feels warm, and won't eat, for instance, or acts listless and drinks a lot more water than usual, at the very least you should take his temperature.

*Second to you, your veterinarian
is your Shar-Pei's best friend.*

You should know your Shar-Pei's normal temperature. The normal body temperature of a Shar-Pei is around 101°F (38.3°C). When the veterinarian takes the puppy's temperature at the first well-puppy checkup, watch the procedure carefully. Ask questions. Then, keep a record of that normal temperature for future reference. This will give you a baseline for future readings. If your suspicions were correct, and the dog does have a fever (generally assumed to be any temperature two degrees Fahrenheit (one degree Celsius) or higher above normal), try to identify other symptoms. Your veterinarian will ask questions about your dog's appetite, general well-being, and recent activities.

Preventive Medicine

Vaccines build up a dog's natural immunity to the bacteria and viruses that cause them

disease. The virus is spread both by direct contact and by airborne particles. It is most common in unvaccinated puppies in the first year of life.

At first, the symptoms of canine distemper resemble a common cold. Because dogs don't catch cold, however, you should be suspicious of any watery discharge from the dog's eyes and nose. Within days, the discharge will turn a thick yellow. Fever, loss of appetite, and listlessness are early symptoms. Later, the dog may have epileptic-type seizures.

The first distemper vaccine should be given shortly after weaning. Because the breeder usually accepts this responsibility, most puppies have their first shots before they go out into the world.

Heartworms

The tragedy of heartworm disease is that it can be prevented. The heartworm larvae, carried by mosquitoes, burrow their way into the dog's system. There the larvae mature into worms that make their way into the dog's heart and lungs. The adult worms live and reproduce for about five years, reaching lengths of 4 to 12 inches (10–30 cm). They entwine around and interfere with the dog's heart valves.

The dog with heartworms doesn't show any symptoms until very late in the disease. At that time, the number one symptom of heartworm infestation is a soft, dry cough. A second indication is the dog's intolerance for exercise. He can't run as fast or as far as he used to. In untreated dogs, the disease may develop into serious and

great pain and frequently shorten their lives. Boosters keep vaccine levels active.

For puppies born to recently vaccinated parents, a possible schedule would be:

✔ eight weeks—canine distemper, hepatitis, leptospirosis, parainfluenza, parvovirus (DHLPP);

✔ twelve weeks—DHLPP (heartworm preventive medication upon veterinarian's recommendation); and

✔ sixteen weeks—DHLPP, rabies.

Canine Distemper

Distemper is the leading cause of infectious death in dogs. It is a highly contagious viral even fatal complications involving the heart, liver, and kidney.

A monthly tablet, not only will protect against heartworms, but also will protect the dog against another parasite, the common hookworm.

Leptospirosis

Dogs get leptospirosis from drinking, swimming, or wading in infected water or from eating infected food. The leptospiral bacteria, found in the urine of an infected animal, for instance, can penetrate unbroken skin. The advanced stage of leptospirosis in dogs results in kidney failure.

Due to the leptospirosis vaccine and annual boosters, and to ever-increasing standards in sanitation practices, this disease no longer is common.

The disease is not contagious to humans as such, but it is caused by an infectious agent called a spirochete that can be transmitted to humans and can cause a disease known as Weil's disease.

Kennel Cough

Infectious tracheobronchitis is a highly contagious disease that spreads rapidly through a group of dogs. The disease lasts several weeks. Even though treated, the dog can be left with chronic bronchitis. Several viruses and bacteria have been implicated. The presence of the *Bordetella bronchosepticum* bacterium can be the primary agent.

Canine Hepatitis

Infectious canine hepatitis is a highly contagious disease that can spread to other dogs. Although a dog can have a mild case of hepatitis, the disease also can be deadly and quick act-ing. Untreated, the disease affects the liver, kidneys, and lining of the blood vessels.

In fatal form, the dog suddenly becomes ill, develops bloody diarrhea, collapses, and dies. Puppies show sudden pain and may die before any treatment can be given. Canine hepatitis can be prevented with an appropriate vaccination schedule.

Canine Parvoviral Disease

Parvoviral disease is highly contagious. Observed in the United States only since 1978, the virus is transmitted from one dog to another through contaminated urine and feces. Although dogs of all ages are affected, puppies under five months old have a high mortality to parvovirus. Dogs that recover, however, are immune.

Two forms of the disease have been noted. In one, symptoms include depression, loss of appetite, vomiting, extreme pain, profuse bloody diarrhea, and high fever. The second form affects the dog's heart muscles. A puppy will stop nursing, cry out, and gasp for breath. Death follows soon after. Parvoviral vaccinations must be kept current.

Canine Coronaviral Gastroenteritis

Coronaviral gastroenteritis is another relatively new disease that gained prominence in 1978. The symptoms of coronaviral infection appear suddenly. A dog that seems well one morning can be vomiting that evening. A general deterioration and wasting follows the onset of persistent diarrhea. If treated promptly with fluids and other protective medications, most dogs will recover in four to five days. Dogs can be vaccinated against coronavirus, but repeated vaccinations may be necessary.

Rabies

Rabies affects all warm-blooded animals, including man. The saliva of an infected wild animal, such as a fox, skunk, or bat, transfers the virus through a bite.

Because the rabies virus inflames the dog's brain, a rabid dog probably will undergo a personality change. The dog may act paralyzed. He may cower or try to hide; he may turn violent, run, or foam at the mouth.

In some cases, the dog's saliva can be infectious a week before any symptoms appear. Unless you can safely confine a suspected animal without endangering yourself, don't approach a dog that is acting strange. Call the authorities. By all means, do not kill the animal. Laboratory tests on a dead animal can be misleading.

Although a series of treatments has been developed for humans, rabies can be fatal to humans and dogs alike.

Coat and Skin Problems

Allergic reactions may be hereditary. Chalk up another good reason to purchase from a breeder who has at least one of the parents on hand. Ask questions about skin problems.

Shar-Pei Syndrome

Some of these short-haired friends encounter this problem because their own stiff, sharp hair pricks into the adjacent skin folds. The affected area becomes red and inflamed. The site itches, and subsequently the dog experiences hair loss, infection, and oozing from the site. The dog frequently licks the area, compounding the problem. Treatment involves keeping the problem area clean, out of the reach of the dog's tongue, and clipping or shaving the offending hairs.

Pests

In summer, especially in warmer climates, the flea and tick problem can get out of control. Many home owners resort to chemical sprays and treated collars. Some of these are very effective. Some dogs, however, are allergic to the chemicals. Some are too young; others are too weak.

Fleas: The flea is the most common parasite on dogs. Because the flea lives by feeding on blood, a severe infestation in your pet can cause anemia. Mild flea shampoos and insecticide dips can remove the adult pests, but the effect is short term. A new generation of flea control products administered topically between the dog's shoulder blades will kill any adult flea or tick. The flea life cycle will be disrupted, further enhancing the product's effectiveness. The adult control lasts for one to three months. The secret to flea control, therefore, is to treat the environment.

To be effective, treatment must continue for four weeks. Ask your veterinarian to recommend a proven insecticidal product containing growth regulators, called ovacides, that will wipe out the egg population as well as kill the adult fleas.

Then, embark on a four-week program. On the first and third weeks of the program, shampoo your dog with a good flea shampoo. Then, once a week, for four weeks, wash the dog's bedding. Vacuum the carpet, the furniture, and the drapes. Burn the vacuum bag. Sprinkle the house with the recommended insecticide. Treat the yard. The program is effective.

Your goal: an affectionate, well-socialized, playful pet.

Ticks: Ticks are found in the woods, in the park, and in your backyard. Ticks mate, however, on your dog. Look for the feeding female tick on your dog's ears, under its neck, or between its toes. The female sometimes swells to about the size and color of a bean. When you find the female, look for the male tick. Often referred to as a seed tick, the male is small and flat, and nearby.

First, wear gloves. Dip a cotton applicator in alcohol. Hold it on the female tick's body. Then catch the tick as close to your dog's skin as possible and pull steadily. Examine the tick to be sure you have the head. Lift the male tick off with tweezers. Dab the affected spot with alcohol.

All ticks are capable of transmitting some disease. One, however, the *Ixodes ricinus* tick,

has been the subject of much national press. Spirochetes from this tick can transfer to humans, causing Lyme disease. The illness, named in 1975 for the Connecticut community where the earliest cases were diagnosed, is now the most frequent tick-borne disease in humans.

Mange

There are two types of mange, demodectic (red mange) and sarcoptic. Both are caused by mites. Both cause loss of hair. Demodectic mange usually does not itch. Dogs with sarcoptic mange itch and scratch excessively.

Demodectic mange is caused by a mite that lives in the hair follicles. This mite is present in many dogs and causes problems for only a few.

SHAR-PEI SOUNDBITES

A dog cannot see details or colors as well as humans but can see much better in dim light.

Demodectic mange usually occurs in puppies three to nine months old whose systems lack the proper immune response to the *Demodex canis* mite. Veterinarians suspect that this lack of response is hereditary. Some Shar-Pei seem particularly susceptible to demodectic mange.

The first symptom of the disease is usually hair loss from the face and front legs. As the disease progresses, the hair loss becomes generalized over the entire body. The coat appears "moth-eaten."

Some untreated puppies make spontaneous recoveries when their immune system develops. The forward progress of the disease is aggravated by inappropriate diet, and by any stress that affects the dog's ability to fight the intrusion. Adolescence, a change in habits, a move to a new location, or jealousy can bring on an attack.

Dogs with sarcoptic mange have a distinctive, musty odor. The dog scratches because the female mites burrow into its skin to lay eggs. The ear tips often are affected. In fact, crusty ear tips are a first symptom.

Treatment includes use of an insecticide dip once a week for three to four weeks.

Allergies, Dermatitis, Hot Spots

A dog can be allergic to almost anything. If your Shar-Pei develops blisters, a rash, or rosy skin, be prepared to answer your veterinarian's questions about its environment. Contact allergies to insecticides, detergents, soaps, flea powders and collars, plastic or rubber food dishes, and outdoor carpet dyes are common.

Your Shar-Pei may itch and scratch in annual cycles, more severe in spring and fall. Dogs sneeze and itch in reaction to allergens, just like you do. Many dogs, not just Shar-Pei, are allergic to ragweed, tree pollens, grass, wool, house dust, feathers, and molds.

If Buddy passes gas, has diarrhea, or itches around the anus, suspect food allergies. Dogs can be allergic to such common products as soy, beef, chicken, corn, wheat, egg whites, milk, and fish. The dog's anal sacs may have accumulated fluids that must be pressed or squeezed out.

Hot spots are not uncommon in Shar-Pei. These weeping, painful bare spots on your dog's coat seem to grow before your eyes. See your veterinarian at the first sign of an oozing, crusting lesion.

If your Shar-Pei does itch and scratch excessively, ask your veterinarian about trying one of the new anti-inflammatory agents. Omega-3 and omega-6 are two fatty acids that have been proven to reduce itching by as much as 20 percent. They have few side effects. You will find both on the market as diet additives, in ointments, and in flea collars.

Pyoderma

Pyoderma is a bacterial skin infection. The problem is easily diagnosed because of the skin's moist, red appearance. Often called "fold dermatitis" or "skin-fold pyoderma," the infection is most commonly seen around the facial and tail wrinkles in such breeds as Blood-

The Shar-Pei is particularly prone to skin problems. Check your pet often for signs of trouble.

hounds, Pugs, and, of course, our Shar-Pei. The resultant itching can cause significant discomfort and areas can become infected. Treatment includes a cleansing shampoo, keeping the area dry and in case of infection, use of antibiotics.

Skin Tumors

Check your Shar-Pei at least once a month for skin changes. Older dogs, especially, are prone to tumors. A sore that doesn't heal, or a lump where none should be, is cause to visit your veterinarian. In a female, feel around the breasts. In a male, check the perianal area around the base of the tail. As with humans, early detection of tumors is essential.

Entropion

Entropion, inward rolling eyelids, is a congenital defect common in, but not limited to Shar-Pei. Many breeds such as the Chow Chow, the Bulldog, and the Bloodhound are especially susceptible. This painful predilection is in large part due to the breed's excessive skin folds. Because entropion can cause blindness, and because it is miserable for the unlucky puppy, breeders have worked hard to produce lines free of it. If left untreated, entropion can cause infection, corneal ulcers, and blindness.

Early treatment involves rolling out the affected lids and stitching, or tacking, the lids into place to keep the eyelashes from brushing the cornea. Because the puppy usually is returned to the litter, and because his skin is extremely fragile, some veterinary ophthalmologists encase the sutures in plastic tubing to distribute the suture pressure. Others tack plastic shirt buttons to the last stitch to achieve the same end result. The puppy is watched carefully. The hope is that the eye tacking will buy time for the puppy to outgrow the problem.

By the time the puppy is six months old, if eye tacking has not taken care of the problem, a more permanent treatment is scheduled. Surgery for adult entropion is performed under a general anesthetic. Slivers of the eyelid tissue are removed and the incision is joined, thus making a permanent "tuck" in the eyelid.

Miscellaneous Problems

Familial Shar-Pei Fever

An inherited inflammatory disorder. The fever, generally lasting 12 to 36 hours, can spike to

prone to renal amyloidosis, an often fatal defect in the breed.

In familial renal amyloidosis, the body's waste materials build up and, if the materials are not removed or filtered, they change and crystallize. At this point, the crystallized fibers will affect whatever organ they enter. The kidney is the most common site of deposit. Kidney failure leads to uremic poisoning. Symptoms can include fever, vomiting, blood in the urine, and back pain. Treatment is usually of the symptoms to keep the dog comfortable.

Patellar Luxation

Patellar luxation (slipped kneecap) can be hereditary or a result of an injury. Luxation means "out of place." In patellar luxation, the ligaments holding the kneecap have slipped and the kneecap is dislocated. It can affect one or both legs. The dog limps, having difficulty straightening the knee. The condition usually can be corrected by surgery.

Otitis Externa

Check your pet's ears weekly for cleanliness or any foreign matter. The small opening to the Shar-Pei's ear canal reduces air circulation and permits bacterial growth. Be sure to dry the ears well after bathing and after any water activity. Use a small towel or cotton ball, not a cotton swab. Despite your precautions, should your Shar-Pei seem to spend a lot of time scratching or rubbing an ear or if you notice any swelling or abnormal odors or discharge and if you are not allowed to touch, you should suspect otitis externa.

107°F (101° to 102.5° is normal). A common side effect, known as Swollen Hock Syndrome, involves a swelling of the joint above the pastern on the back legs. Swelling also can occur on the wrists and even on the lips. Dogs with swollen hocks are extremely uncomfortable, reluctant to move and exhibit a characteristic "walking on eggs" gait when forced to do so. This is a painful condition for which your veterinarian should be consulted.

Shar-Pei that inherit familial Shar-Pei fever may also develop amyloidosis, a build-up of waste products affecting many organs but most often the kidneys. Shar-Pei seem particularly

Megaesophagus

This genetic malady is an abnormality involving the "food tube" or esophagus. The affected dog regurgitates undigested food usually within an hour of eating. Seven breeds are more commonly afflicted: the Shar-Pei, German Shepherds, Great Danes, Greyhounds, Irish Setters, Miniature Schnauzers and Wire-haired Fox Terriers.

Some puppies outgrow the problem, some benefit by eating from a raised food bowl and some by a change to a soft diet.

Bloat

An estimated 60,000 dogs a year are affected with a life-threatening medical emergency known as bloat. Bloat is rare in dogs under age two. Bloat is the result of two factors. First, an overdistention of the stomach has occurred. The distention could have been the result of various causes. Perhaps the dog ate too much, ate too rapidly, swallowed too much air, or exercised too quickly after eating. Second, the stomach's supporting ligaments relaxed, allowing the stomach to rotate, twisting and closing off the stomach valves.

The symptoms occur rapidly. The dog is uncomfortable, paces, and has stomach spasms. He pants, whines, and retches without producing vomit. The dog will go into shock. It is imperative that the dog receive veterinary care within 30 minutes to an hour. As many as 68 percent of affected dogs die. The risk increases with age and weight.

Diarrhea, Vomiting

An occasional soft stool isn't a cause for worry. A dog will get diarrhea as a result of indiscreet eating. Garbage, milk, rich food, a change in diet, and toxic plants often have a laxative effect.

If your dog has mild diarrhea, try cutting back on his food. Offer only dry kibble. Continued diarrhea is serious. If the symptoms have not disappeared by the next day, take your dog to the veterinarian.

Occasional vomiting normally means that the dog has swallowed something that disagreed with him, and is expelling the contents of his stomach. A rule of thumb is, if your dog throws up once or twice and then acts normal, he is probably okay. If vomiting persists, however, call your veterinarian.

Constipation

Most healthy dogs have one or two stools a day. To qualify as constipation, a dog should have difficulty passing a stool. He could show signs of pain. If small, hard stools are normal for your dog and not painful, you should have no worry. Try switching to another kibble. Or add a little bran cereal, celery, or whole wheat bread to your dog's diet.

Sometimes an older male has difficulty because an enlarged prostate bulges into the anal canal. This is a situation for your veterinarian.

Worms

Most puppies are born with worms. Deworming should be done on each litter at two to three weeks of age, and again at five to six weeks. Many adult dogs are subject to worms. Because adult roundworms are very hardy and can live for months or years in soil, some breeders routinely deworm their adult dogs once a year.

Hip Dysplasia

According to the Orthopedic Foundation for Animals (OFA), canine hip dysplasia is an inherited disease resulting in instability of the hip joint.

How Old Is My Shar-Pei in People Years?

Veterinarians, Purdue University researchers, and even the *Farmer's Almanac* have debunked the "age times seven" rule of thumb, suggesting that for a medium-size dog like the Shar-Pei, the table below is more accurate.

Dog's Age	Human's Age
1 year	15 years
2 years	24 years
4 years	32 years
7 years	45 years
10 years	56 years
15 years	76 years
20 years	98 years

The OFA, a not-for-profit foundation, functions as a diagnostic service, evaluates the dog's hip joint status as revealed in a radiograph, and maintains a breed registry.

In December 2004, the OFA issued a summary of tests conducted over the past 30 years. Of the 8,541 Shar-Pei evaluated during that period only 13% were dysplastic. Because good Shar-Pei breeders have their dogs evaluated and remove suspected carriers from their lines, the breed is ranked as low as 65th out of 127 breeds tested.

Home Treatments

Taking Your Dog's Temperature

Shake down a plastic rectal thermometer. Lubricate it, and lift the dog's tail. With a twisting motion, insert the thermometer a couple of inches into the anal canal. Hold the thermometer in place for three minutes. Remove, wipe clean, and read. Normally, a dog's temperature is between 100 to 102°F (37.8–38.9°C). If your dog's temperature rises two degrees Fahrenheit (one degree Celsius) above normal, call your veterinarian.

How to Give Medicine

If you have to give your pet a pill, you might take advantage of a dog's tendency to bolt his food. Coat the pill with peanut butter or wrap it in cheese. Offer one piece of plain peanut butter, for instance, and the coated capsule the next time. The dog probably will swallow it happily.

Otherwise, place the pill in the middle and well to the back of your Shar-Pei's mouth. Hold his jaws together with one hand and gently stroke his throat with the other. You should see a swallow. Praise. Be observant because Shar-Pei are wonderfully adept at concealing the pill and spitting it back at you later.

Liquid medicine is best poured into a lip pocket. Ask someone to help you the first few times until you and the dog get the hang of it. Let the assistant hold the bottle and dropper or spoon. Calm your dog. Make him sit. Tilt his head back.

Using your fingers, pull out the dog's lower lip at the corner where the upper and lower lips join. Have your assistant pour the medicine into this nice, convenient pouch. The medicine should dribble between the teeth and down the throat. Praise your dog.

Weighing Your Shar-Pei

Because accurate dosage depends on the dog's weight, you often will have to know how

Always keep your veterinarian's number on hand in case of an emergency.

much your dog weighs. It is not easy to get your Shar-Pei on a scale.

A simple solution is to step on the scale alone. Weigh yourself. Read the scale and write down the numbers. Bend over and pick up your Shar-Pei. Weigh both of you. Read the scale. The difference in the two figures is the dog's weight.

Emergencies

Emergencies are sudden illnesses or traumas that require immediate care. You should be familiar with some animal aid techniques to help you stabilize your pet until a veterinarian can be called.

Shock

A dog will go into shock just like people do. Any severe trauma such as broken bones, internal injury, or copious bleeding, can send a dog into shock. When the dog's circulation slows, his vital organs don't get enough oxygen. The body temperature lowers, the dog shivers and is weak. His legs and feet chill. Prolonged shock can cause death.

Get help. While waiting, speak soothingly to the dog. Cover him. If you have to move the dog (out of the road, for instance), be careful. An injured dog given further pain will snap and bite.

Snakebites and Stinging Insects

Inquisitive Shar-Pei often will bat at a snake or a lizard. Even a nonpoisonous snakebite can be painful. Bites most often occur on the nose, tongue, or face. A bite on the head can swell alarmingly. In fact, you should suspect snakebite

if the swelling is obvious and grows as you watch it. Get the dog to the veterinarian immediately. Your veterinarian probably has on hand the antivenin for the poisonous snakes in your area. For the best chance of recovery, the antivenin should be given within two hours.

Rarely is the actual spider, bee, or wasp sting observed. Our first indication of a sting is a fast and localized swelling, often on an ear flap. A spider bite results in an intense itching, which doesn't subside for 8 to 12 hours. A bee will leave a stinger behind, which you must pull out with tweezers or your fingernails. In some instances, however, the actual location of the bite may never be determined.

After any insect sting, watch your dog carefully. Provided that the dog is not having a severe reaction, apply a paste of baking soda

Overall good health and obedience should be the long-term goal.

and calamine lotion. Your pet probably would appreciate an ice pack. Within two hours, if the swelling has not subsided, or your dog is still in obvious pain, contact your veterinarian.

Poisoning

The symptoms of poisoning are pain, panting, shivering, lethargy, convulsions, and coma. If your dog hasn't been out of the yard, look to your own garden. Could it have chewed plants that you sprayed recently? Could he have followed you around the yard and gulped slug bait? Does your car engine leak? That sweet-tasting antifreeze on the driveway is poisonous. If you suspect poisoning, get your pet to the veterinarian immediately.

Bleeding and Fractures

The best treatment for bleeding is to apply pressure enroute to a veterinarian. As a last resort, apply a tourniquet between the injury and the heart. If you can reach the veterinarian within 30 minutes, you probably can leave the tourniquet on. Otherwise, loosen the tourniquet for two to three minutes every 30 minutes.

A dog that has been hit by a car can have massive internal injuries. A dog that tangles with a bicycle or one that falls off a porch might be lucky enough to sustain only a fracture. A broken leg is the most common fracture. Keep in mind that the leg will have to be set professionally. Your problem is to get the dog to a veterinarian with as little trauma as possible.

If you suspect a fracture, try to keep the dog calm. A snapped bone grinding against muscle can cause extensive damage. Try not to move the dog until you can get a splint on the leg. Straighten the leg as much as you can. Use whatever is on hand—a yardstick, broom handle, magazine, or heavy cardboard tube—to immobilize the limb. Wrap the splint with gauze, torn strips of cotton, anything handy. Call your veterinarian immediately.

The Elderly Shar-Pei

Aging is a gradual degenerative process as organs and metabolism slow down. As the dog ages, hardening of the arteries puts a burden on his heart. Cancer, heart disease, and kidney disease are his enemies.

Buddy's behavior changes. He seeks warmer spots to sleep, and often loses bladder control. You will find that he is less surefooted and has lost joint flexibility. His bones have become thinner and more brittle. His coat will thin, his epidermis will thin, and damaged hair will regrow at a slower rate. His vision, hearing, and senses of smell and taste slowly ebb.

Older dogs can be kept very comfortable with modern techniques and drugs designed to ease the creaks and groans of age. Pet owners can do their part. Be patient with your old friend. See that your pet has a warm place to sleep in winter and a cool, shaded area in summer. Add a soft pillow to his bed. Try not to make sudden dietary changes. Keep your pet on a low protein, low fat, high fiber diet to control obesity. See that he receives moderate exercise every day to maintain joint flexibility. Don't change his daily routine. Avoid the stress of unnecessary travel and unfamiliar sleeping arrangements. Keep all shots up-to-date. And above all, don't let an older pet run loose near traffic. Hearing goes before sight and smell.

The question of euthanasia is painful. The pain of an animal who can find no relief from his suffering is pitiable. Many animal lovers

SHAR-PEI SOUNDBITES

The wrinkles on the Shar-Pei's forehead are said to resemble the Chinese characters for "Longevity."

believe that an animal living in misery should be allowed a final rest.

When the time comes that your friend can find no relief from his suffering, it is time to say good-bye. Your veterinarian has access to several drugs, which, when injected, put your pet to sleep in a matter of seconds. If you are there, a friend to the end, that end is peaceful and without pain.

Keep your older dog as comfortable as possible.

Organizations

The Chinese Shar-Pei Club of America
Secretary, Jo Ann Redditt
3510 Washington Court
Alexandria, VA 22302
www.cspca.com

American Kennel Club (AKC)
5580 Centerview Drive
Raleigh, NC 27606-3390
919-233-9767
www.akc.org

Periodicals

The Barker
Marge B. Calltharp, Editor
44 Mt. Parnassus Rd.
P.O. Box 241
East Haddam, CT 06423
TheBarker@Adelphia.net

AKC Gazette
5580 Centerview Drive
Raleigh, NC 27606-3390
919-233-9767
orderdesk@akc.org

Books

Ackerman, Lowell, DVM. *Shar-Pei.* Neptune City, NJ: TFH, 1996.
Coile, D. Caroline. *Encyclopedia of Dog Breeds.* Hauppauge, NY: Barron's Educational Series, Inc., 2005.
Cunliffe, Juliette. *Chinese Shar-Pei.* Allenhurst, NJ: Kennel Club Books, 2000.
Redditt, Jo Ann. *The Chinese Shar-Pei,* New York: Howell, 1996.

Videos

Chinese Shar-Pei AKC Standard Video
5580 Centerview Drive
Raleigh, NC 27606-3390
919-233-9767

Children and puppies can be a great fit.

Despite their "fighting dog" history, Shar-Pei can make excellent family pets.

Internet
Chinese Shar-Pei Club of America
www.cspca.com

The Chinese Shar-Pei Search Engine
www.sharpei.com/au

Dr. Jeff Vidt's Shar-Pei Website
www.drjwv.com

American Dog Trainers
www.inch.com/~dogs/travel.html

Pet Registries
AKC: 1-800-252-7894 or *www.akccar.org*

HomeAgain: 1-866-PET ID-24 or
   www.homeagainID.com

About the Author

The Dog Writers' Association of America awarded its coveted Maxwell medal to the first edition of Mrs. Ditto's *Shar-Pei* book naming it best in its category. An active member of Pensacola Dog Fanciers and specific breed clubs, Mrs. Ditto currently resides in Gulf Breeze, Florida. The author also penned Barron's *Dalmatians* and Barron's *English Springer Spaniels*.

Cover Photos

Front and Back covers: Isabelle Francais; inside front and back cover: Pets by Paulette.

Photo Credits

Isabelle Francais: TOC, pages 4, 9, 31, 34, 43, 46, 49, 50 (top), 52, 53, 78, 83, 92; Pets by Paulette: pages 5, 6, 11, 12, 15, 18, 19, 22, 23, 24, 27, 28, 32, 33, 35, 37, 48, 50 (bottom), 51, 54, 58, 61, 65, 66, 67, 71, 72, 74, 80, 85, 86, 89, 90; Kent Dannen: 7, 14, 17, 20, 25, 29, 39, 45, 47, 59, 60, 69, 73, 79, 91, 93; Tara Darling: 13, 40, 62; Norvia Behling: 21

Important Note

This guide tells the reader how to buy and care for a Shar-Pei. The advice given in the book primarily concerns normally developed puppies from a good breeder in excellent physical condition and of good character.

Anyone who adopts a fully grown dog should be aware that the animal has already formed its basic impression of human beings. The new owner should watch the animal carefully, including its behavior toward humans, and should meet the previous owner.

Caution is further advised in the association of children with dogs, in meeting with other dogs, and in exercising the dog without a leash.

Even well-behaved and carefully supervised dogs sometimes do damage to someone else's property or cause accidents. It is therefore in the owner's interest to be adequately insured against such eventualities. We strongly urge all dog owners to purchase a liability policy that covers their dogs.

A Note from the Author

Throughout this book, the pronouns "he" and "she" have been used in alternating chapters to refer to the fictional "Buddy" and "Princess." No gender bias is intended by this writing style.

All inquiries should be addressed to:
Barron's Educational Series, Inc.
250 Wireless Boulevard
Hauppauge, NY 11788
www.barronseduc.com

ISBN-13: 978-0-7641-2849-3
ISBN-10: 0-7641-2849-3

Library of Congress Catalog Card No. 2005051212

Library of Congress Cataloging-in-Publication Data
Ditto, Tanya B.
   Shar-Pei : everything about purchase, care, nutrition, behavior, and training: with a special chapter on understanding the Shar-Pei / Tanya B. Ditto ; color photos by well-known photographers and drawings by Michele Earle-Bridges.
      p. cm. — (Complete pet owner's manual)
   Includes index.
   ISBN-13: 978-0-7641-2849-3
   ISBN-10: 0-7641-2849-3
      1. Chinese Shar-Pei. I. Title. II. Series.

SF429.C48D58   2006
639.76—dc22   2005051212

Printed in China
9 8 7 6 5 4 3 2 1